MARY SHELLEY

by William A. Walling

In *Mary Shelley* the author has attempted to do justice to a writer who had the misfortune--at least in a literary sense--of being the wife of a much greater artist than herself. The author of six novels, Mary Shelley is a more substantial author in the first three of them than is generally recognized. *Frankenstein* (1818), of course, is one of the best known works from the Romantic period in England. But in Mary's second novel, *Valperga* (1823), she produced a lively, highly readable significant criticism of the ideal of military heroism. In her third novel, *The Last Man* (1826), Mary was even more successful. Drawing upon the theme of the desolation of the earth by a plague, she created an oddly disturbing work whose symbolic structure implies a radical criticism of nineteenth-century liberalism.

In her editorial labors as well Mary Shelley has at times been unjustly treated. Although by twentieth-century standards her handling of Shelley's poetry and prose is extremely faulty, too often her modern critics forget the human context in which her editorial work was done. Often sick, pressed by financial worries, working with the manuscripts not of a long-dead author but of the man who had fathered her four children, Mary Shelley performed the greatest service possible to Shelley's memory: she insured that the work he had done would survive so that better trained and more objective editors might establish definitive texts.

In short, this study is to place Mary Shelley as accurately as possible within the context of her own time and of ours. Indisputably she is a minor figure, but the underlying assumption of *Mary Shelley* is that she is one of those minor figures who cannot be discounted in the assessment of an age.

...UTHORS SERIES

...E. Bowman, Editor

INDIANA UNIVERSITY

Mary Shelley

...AUTHOR

...liam A. Walling received his ...New York University. He has ...William Blake, Henry Fielding, ...completed four chapters of a ...istorical development of major ...s (to be published in the fall ...spent 1969-1970 as a Fulbright ...he University of Algiers, and ...has been working on a short ...rd-world cinema which is a ...wth of his Fulbright year. ...associate professor of English ...College, Rutgers (New Bruns- ...serves as associate chairman of ...nt.

Mary Shelley

By WILLIAM A. WALLING

Rutgers—The State University

MARY SHELLEY

Preface

The problem in any serious study of Mary Shelley is twofold. Although she produced a fairly large body of work, her literary reputation rests almost entirely on a single novel, *Frankenstein;* and although she possessed, as much as any other writer, her own particular sensibility, she was first the mistress, then the wife, and finally the widow of a poet whose own career has received a staggering amount of attention. Consequently, there is usually to be found in treatments of Mary a bias, more or less obvious, in either of two directions: (1) to treat her work after *Frankenstein* (with the exception of her notes on Shelley's poetry and prose) as a tiresome mass of wasted effort; or (2) to regard her as an occasionally interesting but distinctly minor appendage whose writings derive their chief importance from the fact that they reflect something of the vitality of Shelley and his circle. (Even in what is perhaps the single most helpful book yet published on Mary Shelley, Elizabeth Nitchie's *Mary Shelley: Author of Frankenstein* (1953), we find this general summation of Mary's value: "At the very least, her novels and tales are *romans à clef* which furnish the fun of identity spotting. At best they present characters that take on something of the actuality of the real persons who were their models" [140].)

Yet such a dual tendency has obscured for too long the true outlines of Mary's own significance as a writer. And the organization of this study has been determined by the belief that her first three novels ought to earn for Mary Shelley a higher position than she currently holds in the literary history of the early nineteenth century. Thus, although the importance of *Frankenstein* is recognized by the length and position of the chapter which is devoted to it (Chapter 2), both *Valperga* and *The Last Man,* her second and third novels, also receive detailed discussions in chapters of their own. Furthermore, the attempt has been made in the latter chapters to devote adequate attention to every area of Mary's writing which might possibly have a bearing on an understanding of her total achievement, including, for example, a brief discussion of the relatively neglected five volumes of *Lives* she wrote for Lardner's *Cabinet Cyclopedia* in the 1830's; as well as a general consideration of her role as Shelley's editor, an aspect of her work which has recently received a good deal of attention.

Last of all, although it is obvious that the enormous shadow cast by Shelley has been responsible for a good deal of the climate of disparagement and underestimation in which Mary's reputation subsists, it would be fatuous to attempt to ignore him in any study of her writings. As a result, I have not hesitated to touch upon his work in relationship to hers whenever I felt some significant insight might be gained. At the same time, I hope the Shelley specialist will recognize that in a study as brief as this one, devoted as it is not to Shelley but to his wife, references to so highly complex a mind as his must of necessity suffer from the danger of oversimplification and excessive compression.

I owe thanks to the following people and institutions: to the Research Council at Rutgers for a grant which aided in the preparation of the manuscript; to Professor Kenneth Neill Cameron, both as a teacher and a friend, for having dispelled a good many of my illusions about the Romantic period; to the staffs at the New York Public Library, the Princeton University Library, and the Rutgers Library both at Douglass and at the College of Arts and Science; to the many scholars upon whose work I have drawn both consciously and otherwise in the following pages (most especially to the late Elizabeth Nitchie and to Professor Frederick L. Jones); to Mrs. Paula Horvath for her labors with an often difficult manuscript; to Professor Sylvia Bowman for her editorial help; and finally, and most importantly, to my wife for her generous patience with a very slow writer.

WILLIAM WALLING

Rutgers University

Contents

Chronology

1797   On March 29, William Godwin and Mary Wollstonecraft marry at Old St. Pancras Church, London, their intimacy having begun in the summer of the preceding year. Five months later, on August 30, at 11:20 P.M., Mary is born. On September 10, Mary Wollstonecraft dies as a result of the aftereffects of childbirth.

1801   On December 21, Godwin marries for the second time. His wife, a Mrs. Mary Jane Clairmont, brings with her a son (Charles), a daughter (Jane), and a doubtful past.

1805   Godwin, at his wife's persuasion, begins a publishing firm specializing in children's books, the Juvenile Library. This venture involves Mary's father in endless financial difficulties.

1807   The Godwin household moves to 41 Skinner Street, Snow Hill.

1812   On June 7, Godwin sends Mary to live in Dundee with the family of a Scottish friend, William Baxter. On November 11, Mary, back in London for a visit with one of the Misses Baxters, meets Shelley and his wife Harriet at Skinner Street.

1814   On March 30, Mary returns to Skinner Street, her Scottish residence ended. There, on May 5, she meets Shelley again. By June 26, Shelley has declared his love; and on July 28, Mary and Shelley elope, Jane (eventually to become Claire) Clairmont—Mary's "stepsister"—accompanying them. The three travel through France, Switzerland, Germany, and Holland, returning to England on September 14. This trip is the basis for the first part of *History of a Six Weeks' Tour*, published anonymously in 1817.

1815   Mary's first child, a girl, is born prematurely on February 22 and dies March 6. In August, Mary and Shelley move to Bishopgate and remain there until May 1816.

1816   On January 24, Mary bears Shelley a son, William, named in honor of Godwin. Mary, Shelley, and Claire leave for Geneva in May. In June or July, Mary begins working on *Frankenstein*. She returns to England with Shelley on August 29. On December 10, Harriet Shelley is found drowned in the Serpentine; on December 30, Mary and Shelley marry at St. Mildred's, Bread Street, London.

1817   Mary and Shelley take up residence at Marlow in March and remain there until the following year. On September 2, Mary gives birth to a daughter, Clara Everina.

1818   On March 11, *Frankenstein* is published; Mary and Shelley leave for Italy. On September 24, Clara dies at Venice.

1819   Mary and Shelley reside in Rome from March to June. On June 7, William dies. In early November, Mary completes her *novella, Mathilda,* unpublished in her lifetime. On November 12, at Florence, she gives birth to a son, Percy Florence.

1822   Shelley and Edward Williams are drowned on July 8. Soon afterward Mary writes her poem, "The Choice."

1823   On February 6, Sir Timothy Shelley writes to Byron to offer to assume the guardianship of Percy Florence. Mary refuses the offer on February 25. *Valperga* is published in the same month. On August 25, she returns to England.

1824   On April 19, Byron dies. Shortly after June 1, Mary's edition of Shelley's *Posthumous Poems* is published. Sir Timothy objects strongly; by August 22, after the sale of more than three hundred copies, Mary agrees to suppress the remainder.

1826   *The Last Man* is published in February. On September 14, Charles Bysshe Shelley, the child of Harriet and Shelley, dies. Percy Florence thus becomes heir to the title.

1828   Mary has smallpox while in Paris.

1830   *Perkin Warbeck* is published.

1835   *Lodore* is published. Her two volumes of Italian *Lives* appear in Lardner's *Cabinet Cyclopedia.*

1836   Godwin dies on April 7.

1837   *Falkner* is published. A volume of Spanish and Portuguese *Lives* appears in the *Cabinet Cyclopedia.*

1838   The first volume of French *Lives* is published in the *Cabinet Cyclopedia.*

1839   Volume II of the French *Lives* appears. Mary's edition of Shelley's *Poetical Works* is published in four volumes. A second, expanded edition (in one volume) appears in the same year. Mary's edition of Shelley's prose—*Essays, Letters from Abroad, Translations and Fragments* (dated 1840)—is also published.

1844   On April 23, Sir Timothy Shelley dies. Percy Florence succeeds to the title. In July, Mary's account of her Continental travels (in 1840, 1842, and 1843) appears in two volumes, *Rambles in Germany and Italy.*

1848   Mary's letters express consternation about the revolutions of 1848. Sir Percy Florence marries on June 22. His wife, deeply attached to Mary, will do much after her mother-in-law's death to expand upon Mary's memory of Shelley as "a celestial spirit."

1851   On February 1, Mary dies in London.

CHAPTER 1

Introduction

I *General Biography*

PERHAPS no other writer of her generation began life with a more auspicious background for literary achievement than did Mary Shelley. By the time of her birth, August 30, 1797, her father, William Godwin, had already secured a position as one of the most noted authors of the age. His *Enquiry concerning Political Justice,* first published in 1793, had catapulted him into extraordinary fame; and the reputation he had attained so dramatically as a leading political and moral theorist of the radical school was more than sustained in the following year with the publication of a highly successful novel, *Caleb Williams.* Indeed, the conjunction of two such works—one a nearly one-thousand page expression of closely reasoned arguments on the highest moral abstractions; the other, a compelling novel of guilt and pursuit—must have, as Godwin's biographer suggests, reduced Godwin's reading public to a state of wonder at the versatility of the man.[1]

Yet extraordinary as was the father of Mary Shelley, her mother Mary Wollstonecraft was, in her own way, surely as notable. The author of *A Vindication of the Rights of Woman* (1792), a book which, in its sustained espousal of the principle of sexual equality, proved her "the most fearlessly intelligent woman of her time—and perhaps the greatest,"[2] Mary Wollstonecraft was a figure who, through ability and personality, had achieved a marked eminence in London literary society. Robert Southey, for example, declared in 1801 that he had "never praised [a] living being yet, except Mary Wollstonecraft,"[3] while many of the greatest figures of the age were her personal acquaintances—men such as William Blake, Thomas Paine, Richard Price, Henry Fuseli, and Jacques Pierre Brissot.[4] Surely such a mother as this one and such a father as William Godwin could hardly fail to produce a most exceptional child.

But whatever the intellectual advantages Mary Shelley may be said to have possessed by virtue of her parentage, her childhood—and in that sense her entire destiny—was profoundly affected by the death of her mother soon after Mary's birth. Incalculable in its far-reaching effect, the bald outline of Mary Wollstonecraft's decline is easy enough to trace. A labor of eighteen hours, a failure on the physician's part to extract all of the placenta, the calling in of another, less experienced physician, the onset of shivering fits due to infection—the dreaded result was swift and irrevocable. By the morning of September 10, less than two weeks after parturition, Mary Wollstonecraft was dead.[5] The little girl whose birth had been the unwitting agent of death was to remain motherless until the end of 1801, when Godwin married for the second time.

The problem of the character of the second Mrs. Godwin, Mrs. Mary Jane Clairmont, need not detain us long. Whether she was indeed the "Bitch" of Charles Lamb's report, or the "amiable woman" that Aaron Burr found,[6] the strong distaste Mary Shelley herself expressed for her stepmother in later years suggests how unhappy was the choice (from Mary's point of view) that Godwin had made in choosing a "widow"[7] with two children of her own. For, although it would be naïve to imagine that Godwin's second marriage introduced Mary to anything even remotely resembling the fairy-tale world of the cruel stepmother, there are clues enough to indicate the undoubted resentment Mary experienced in a home which, by 1803, contained five children of assorted parentage: Fanny Imlay (born in 1794), the illegitimate daughter of Mary Wollstonecraft and Gilbert Imlay; Mary herself; Charles (born in 1795) and Jane (born in 1798), the two children of Mrs. Clairmont; and the infant William, born in 1803, the only child in the miscellany to have both his parents rear him. Thus Mary, once she was free of her home, referred to the second Mrs. Godwin as "that filthy woman,"[8] or that "odious" creature,[9] claiming that she felt "something analogous to disgust" at the mere mention of her name[10]—a bitterness so intense as to compel our assent to Elizabeth Nitchie's suggestion that the brief sketch of the Derham marriage in *Lodore* (1835) must indicate something of Mary's verdict on her father's choice.[11] For in that novel we learn that Mrs. Derham was "illiterate and vulgar [and] coarse-minded," so grossly unequal to the studious Mr. Derham that it was a matter of "excessive wonder" why he had ever married her.[12]

That this assessment by a resentful stepdaughter is manifestly unfair—as least as to the illiteracy[13]—is not the point, of course. What matters is the subjective reality of what Mary must often have felt: her sense of isolation (no doubt even then intense and chronic) in a home whose female head evidently favored her own daughter, Jane.[14] There is even, in a pair of letters from Mary's later years, strong indications of a situation which must have contributed to the increasing tension between her and her stepmother. In 1822, Mary declared that, until she had met Shelley, her father "was my God—and I remember many childish instances of the excess of attachment I bore for him."[15] And twelve years later, in 1834, she confided to an old friend about the "excessive and romantic attachment to my Father" which the second Mrs. Godwin "had discovered" when Mary was still quite young.[16]

Surely in these remarks we have an indication of a somewhat unhealthy, if hardly unusual, rivalry between the blossoming young girl and the aging second wife (Mrs. Godwin herself painfully aware that her physical attractions had faded)[17] for the dominant place in Godwin's affections. Perhaps even, although here we tread on more treacherous ground, we have the psychological foundation for Mary's recurrent theme of an only daughter reared, in the absence of a mother, by a loving father figure—the theme receiving its baldest expression in *Mathilda* (written in 1819), a *novella* depicting a father's incestuous desire for his daughter.

At any rate, a few months before Mary's fifteenth birthday, Godwin sent her to Scotland, partly for her health, as we know,[18] but also, one cannot help suspecting, for a more secure domestic peace. This second reason, invariably treated rather superficially by biographers, seems probable on the face of the available evidence. In June, 1811, exactly one year before Mary departed for Scotland, her stepmother suggested to Godwin that Mary remain at Ramsgate while the rest of the family return to London;[19] in 1812, with Mary apparently already in Scotland, Godwin described her to a correspondent as "singularly bold" and as "somewhat imperious"[20] and, in the latter part of the same year, Harriet Shelley furnished an invaluable glimpse of the genuine pathos of Mrs. Godwin's situation: Mary, she tells a friend, "is very much like her mother, whose picture hangs up in [Godwin's] study. She must have been a most lovely woman."[21] Indeed, in 1819, when Mary herself came to write *Mathilda,* she describes her youthful and motherless heroine (an obvious self-portrait) as pining away "in

Scotland" for the sight of her father and as constantly dreaming of running away in disguise to search him out.[22]

But whatever this assorted bag of hints may suggest about the state of Mary's emotions in Scotland, the undisputed fact is that she remained there for nearly two years, from the summer of 1812 until the early spring of 1814, and returned to London in the interim for only occasional, short visits. Of that Scottish stay Mary was to write in later years that it was "beneath the trees of the grounds belonging to our house, or on the bleak sides of the woodless mountains near, that my true compositions, the airy flights of my imagination, were born and fostered."[23] Yet valuable as this sojourn was for Mary, what was infinitely more significant for her career were the events which soon followed her return to London on March 30, 1814.

She had met Percy Bysshe Shelley earlier, in November, 1812, on one of her visits home from Scotland; but at that time the poet was still emotionally at rest in his marriage to Harriet Westbrook. By the spring of 1814 the situation between husband and wife had altered radically. Due partly to Harriet's refusal to nurse their child herself, partly to the interference of her sister, possibly (but I think improbably) to Harriet's relations with a Major Ryan, but most of all to Shelley's own restless nature, a serious rift had developed in the marriage. In addition, and this fact is perhaps of equal importance, Mary was no longer the fourteen-year-old girl of 1812. Almost seventeen by the time the two of them met again in May, she had grown into an extremely attractive young woman who was the aptly fitting daughter (in Shelley's eyes) of Mary Wollstonecraft, whose portrait, as we have seen, hung prominently in the Godwin home. Indeed, the fact that Mary had had such a mother undoubtedly played its part in Shelley's interest in her:

> They say that thou wert lovely from thy birth,
> Of glorious parents, thou aspiring Child.
> I wonder not—for One then left this earth
> Whose life was like a setting planet mild,
> Which clothed thee in the radiance undefiled
> Of its departing glory.
>
> ("Dedication: To Mary," *The Revolt of Islam*)

And we can hardly be surprised, granted Shelley's nature and the published Godwinian view of marriage, that an attachment grew rapidly. By June 26, Shelley had declared his love; by June 27, an intimacy seems to have begun; and, by the following month, Mary was pregnant. The two eloped on the morning of July 28, and Jane (later to call herself "Claire") Clairmont, Mary's "step-sister," accompanied the runaway couple in their flight to the Continent.

The elopement, of course, was the single most important event of Mary Shelley's career. With it, at one stroke, she passed from a teen-aged dependence in a home hopelessly burdened with financial worries to a full-fledged participation in a much larger life. With it, too, her uncertain early efforts at writing were given a powerful push forward; for Shelley had little doubt that Mary possessed extraordinary gifts. He eagerly anticipated reading the apprentice work she had done before their intimacy had begun,[24] seems to have been instrumental in motivating her soon afterward to begin a novel called (oddly enough for a lovers' journey) "Hate,"[25] "was forever inciting [her] to obtain literary reputation,"[26] and played the role of active collaborator in Mary's first published volume— *History of a Six Weeks' Tour* (1817). In truth, even *Frankenstein,* the novel by which Mary Shelley's name most surely survives, would never have been begun without the stimulus of Shelley and his friends.[27]

And yet, paradoxically, despite the undoubted impetus life with Shelley gave to Mary's career as a writer, we can see in retrospect that the elopement also had its profoundly adverse effect. As one of Mary's early biographers points out, "Mary's life reached its zenith too suddenly, and with happiness came care in undue proportion. The future of intellectual expansion and creation which might have been hers was not to be fully realized."[28] For it is too easily forgotten in assessments of Mary's stature as a writer (or lack of it) how extraordinary it was that she was able to achieve any literary eminence at all. Before she was twenty, she had given birth to three children. Before she was twenty-two, she had lost all of them. And, although the same year (1819) was to see the birth of the only child who survived her (Percy Florence), the death of Shelley in 1822 left her an impoverished widow of twenty-four with two responsibilities which, in her psychological reaction to them, far transcended any literary ambitions of her own: the vindication and enlargement of her husband's memory; and the care, maintenance, and advancement of her infant son.

II *Early Apprenticeship: Before Shelley*

From both a biographic and a literary point of view, then, we can conveniently divide Mary's life into three unequal parts: before Shelley, with Shelley, and after Shelley. For the first period, her early apprenticeship in relative isolation either in the heterogeneous Godwin household or with the Baxters in Scotland, little space is needed. "As a child I scribbled," she tells us in her introduction to the 1831 edition of *Frankenstein;* "and my favourite pastime during the hours given me for recreation was to 'write stories.' " In these early efforts, Mary, true to the pattern of most fledgling authors, attempted few original flights of her own: "I was a close imitator—rather doing as others had done than putting down the suggestions of my own mind."[29] Even later, as a girl of fifteen in Scotland where her writing continued, she produced nothing, according to her own account, that had any value. "I wrote then," she admits laconically, "but in a most commonplace style."[30]

Yet however little intrinsic worth these adolescent attempts possessed, there can be no doubt of Mary's industry. A box of her writings accompanied her on her elopment with Shelley; and, although these early manuscripts were lost shortly afterward in Paris, Shelley's comments on them make it clear that they represented a substantial amount of material.[31] At any rate, the first part of Mary's career—her attempts at writing before Shelley became an intimate part of her life—can be described as one of precocious apprenticeship: she wrote a surprising amount for someone so young; little of it, we can assume, was of any value; and all of it, unfortunately, both for the literary critic and for the biographer, has vanished.

III *With Shelley*

Her second period—with Shelley—possesses, in many ways, the greatest literary interest. Shortly after the loss of her early writings in Paris in the summer of 1814, Mary began to write "Hate," a novel which she never finished and which is now, in whatever manuscript length it did attain, also lost. Apparently the novel was begun in emulation of a work of Shelley's, for Mary was giving him editorial and secretarial assistance during this period on a prose fiction of his own, *The Assassins.*[32] But whatever cause lay behind Mary's failure to finish "Hate," her next attempt at an extended work—"The Life of Louvet"—was understandably hampered by her physical condition. Begun on November 12, 1814, when she was already four or five months pregnant,[33] "The Life of Louvet" could have drawn from Mary only the most intermittent of efforts. Again and again her journal bears laconic witness to how unwell she was from November through January; and by the time of the birth—and shortly afterward the death—of a premature girl in early 1815, Mary had surely lost whatever interest she had once possessed for the project.

At this point in her career, we feel for the first time the force of her remark (written in 1831) that with Shelley "life became busier and reality stood in the place of fiction."[34] Indeed, nothing she ever wrote afterward is more genuinely moving than some of the entries in her journal describing her reaction (and she was only a seventeen-year-old girl) to the death of her first child, on March 6, 1815:

Monday, Mar. 6.—Find my baby dead. Send for Hogg. Talk. A miserable day. . . .

Thursday, Mar. 9.—Read and talk. Still think about my little baby. . . .

Monday, Mar. 13.—Shelley and Clara go to town. Stay at home; net, and think of my little dead baby. This is foolish, I suppose; yet whenever I am left alone to my own thoughts, and do not read to divert them, they always come back to the same point—that I was a mother, and am so no longer. . . .

Sunday, Mar. 19.—Dream that my little baby came to life again; that it had been only cold, and that we rubbed it before the fire, and it lived. Awake and find no baby. I think about the little thing all day. Not in good spirits.[35]

"Reality," we see, could be a brutal taskmaster for young women in the early nineteenth century; and Mary Shelley, so clearly and so strongly maternal, was destined to undergo this agony of loss twice more—with a son and with another daughter—before she reached her twenty-third birthday.

Early in 1816 she gave birth to a son, William, named in honor of her father. Some months later, in May, she, Shelley, Claire, and the child departed for the Continent. There, only a short time afterward, she began work on the novel which was to bring her an enduring fame, *Frankenstein. Frankenstein,* however, was not to appear until March, 1818. In the interim, Mary published her first volume—*History of a Six Weeks' Tour*—a brief and engagingly simple account of the elopement journey in 1814, padded out to a small volume by the addition of four letters describing experiences on the Continent in 1816 (two by Mary, two by Shelley) and by Shelley's far-from-simple meditative poem, "Mont Blanc."[36] In all accuracy, then, Mary's first significant publication[37] was a collaborative effort with Shelley.

But *Frankenstein,* of course, brought her genuine recognition. By August, 1818, five months after publication, one of Shelley's friends was able to write from England that the book was "universally known and read";[38] six years later, during a debate in Parliament on the slave trade, George Canning, destined to become prime minister within the decade, illustrated his argument with a flattering reference to *Frankenstein;*[39] Leigh Hunt, in his "Blue Stocking Revels" of 1837, alluded to Mary's fame not only for being the daughter of Mary Wollstonecraft and William Godwin, not merely, in addition, for being the widow of a major poet, but also for having created one of the central characters of the age: "And Shelley, four-famed—for her parents, her lord,/And the poor lone impossible monster abhorred" (11. 209–10). Furthermore, as we know, the title page of each of Mary's subsequent novels was to bear, as an enticement to the reader, a reference to her authorship of *Frankenstein.*

But "reality" again intervened cruelly between the success of her first novel and the completion (in late 1821) of her second, *Valperga.* Living in Italy with Shelley and their two children (a girl, Clara Everina, had been born September 2, 1817), Mary was to watch helplessly while first Clara, and then William died—the girl on September 24, 1818, at Venice; the boy, on June 7, 1819, at Rome. The death of her son struck Mary hardest, for the little boy suffered a lingering death, having first fallen seriously ill on June 2; and, by the time of his death at noon on June 7, Mary herself was prostrate. Her own records of this period speak most poignantly through their silence, for the last entry in her diary is simply *June* 4, with nothing after it, as if she has tried to write but could not; and, on the blank page below the date, we find Shelley's own stark comment: "The journal ends here."[40]

So too, Mary was to write afterward, ended her happiness on that June 7.[41] And, in truth, for some time after the death of William, her letters reflected the terrible shock she had received. To Amelia Curran, she confessed she was unable to keep her thoughts from returning again and again to her lost child;[42] and to Leigh Hunt, who had written a number of times in a vain attempt to lighten her spirits, Mary tried to explain how meaningless her life had become: "The world will never be to me again as it was—there was a life & freshness in it that is lost to me. . . . I ought to have died on the 7th of June last."[43]

With the birth of her fourth and last child, Percy Florence, on November 12, 1819, Mary's spirits revived. Within a few months she was vigorously at work on the research and writing of *Valperga,* bringing that long, underrated novel to completion in the space of two years. Yet, although her son was to live on to a ripe and apparently quite happy old age (he died in December, 1889), Mary soon endured another, this time irremediable, loss. On July 8, 1822, almost midway between the completion of *Valperga* (in late 1821) and its publication (in early 1823), Shelley, along with Edward Williams and Charles Vivian, was drowned in the Bay of Spezzia during a heavy squall.

The second period of Mary Shelley's career then—her life with Shelley—was filled with both personal tragedy and literary success. She published for the first time, in 1817. In 1818 she achieved her greatest popular triumph with *Frankenstein.* By the end of 1821, despite the loss of two more children after the success of *Frankenstein,* she had recovered enough, largely through the birth of her fourth child and the generous encouragement and understanding of Shelley, to complete a second novel—one which (as Shelley realized) was superior in certain ways to her first.

At this point, Mary, only twenty-four, seemed destined for an extraordinary eminence among the writers of the period. From childhood on she had dreamed of achieving fame as a writer. Through her elopement with Shelley she had entered an arena of thought and experience larger perhaps than that of any other woman in England before George Eliot. Her own efforts had secured for her, by her twenty-first birthday, an enviable reputation and a reasonably large following. All that was needed now, it would appear, was simply time enough to bring to fruition the early promise. And yet, of course, the wife of Shelley became too soon the widow of Shelley—a widow, moreover, burdened with a complex and enfeebling reaction to her husband's death,[44] as well as with an infant son whose future depended in large part on the exertions of her pen. As a consequence, the remarkable early promise was never to be fulfilled.

IV *After Shelley*

The third part of Mary's life and career—and the longest— stretches from Shelley's death to her own in early 1851. During it, she produced four novels, five volumes of biographical sketches for Lardner's *Cabinet Cyclopedia,* two volumes of travel writings, a handful of articles and poems, almost a score of short stories, and two brief fragments of biography, one of Godwin, one of Shelley, neither of which, unfortunately, she could bring herself to finish. In addition, she edited Shelley's poetry and prose, supplying with the text a rich store of notes which have proved indispensable to later scholarship. Altogether, the record is one of an essentially brave, undeniably generous, often emotionally confused woman who, much of the time, found herself working (and living) against the grain but who, in spite of this, worked on steadily.

Perhaps a brief examination of the emotional and psychological background to the first novel she wrote after Shelley's death (*The Last Man,* 1826) will make clear something of Mary's condition during this final period of her career. The subject of that novel— the destruction of the human race by plague until only a single survivor remains—coincided closely with the overwhelming sense of isolation Mary herself felt following Shelley's loss. On October 2, 1822, nearly three months after the drowning, she brought herself to write in her journal for the first time:

On the 8th of July I finished my journal. This is a curious coincidence. The date still remains—the fatal 8th—a monument to show that all ended then. And I begin again? Oh, never! . . . I have no friend. For eight years I communicated, with unlimited freedom, with one whose genius, far transcending mine, awakened and guided my thoughts. I conversed with him; rectified my errors of judgment; obtained new lights from him; and my mind was satisfied. Now I am alone—oh, how alone! The stars may behold my tears, and the wind drink my sighs; but my thoughts are a sealed treasure, which can confide to none.[45]

And two years later, with work on the novel apparently well under way, Mary confided to herself: "The last man! Yes, I may well describe that solitary being's feelings, feeling myself as the last relic of a beloved race, my companions extinct before me."[46]

But this sense of hopeless isolation and, it might be charged, of luxurious self-pity was never really allowed to have its full enfeebling effect. Percy Florence also remained, a responsibility which could not be ignored. "Oh, my child!," Mary wrote when she did not yet know what Shelley's father—Sir Timothy—would decide about her and her child's maintenance, "what is your fate to be? You alone reach me; you are the only chain that links me to time; but for you I should be free."[47] And "free," indeed, she was not to be; for the harshness of Sir Timothy's refusal to provide any help unless she would surrender Percy Florence to his care threw Mary back decisively on her own resources.

In 1823, she returned to England, hoping that her presence there with her child would soften Sir Timothy's attitude.[48] In the meantime, while she awaited that desired result, she was confident that she would be able to support herself by her own writings and by "Shelley's Mss."[49] Unfortunately, an ironic impasse developed in which the partial success of her first plan—the gaining of a small allowance from Sir Timothy[50]—was counterbalanced by the partial thwarting of the second; for the old man desired that his errant son's name be forgotten as soon as possible. Thus, Mary's first venture with "Shelley's Mss." proved nearly abortive; for, when her edition of the *Posthumous Poems* appeared in 1824, it was met by Sir Timothy's swift, indignant reaction. Threatening to discontinue any further shows of help, he demanded that the edition be suppressed, that the remaining copies (191 out of an original run of 500) be placed in the hands of a third party, and that Mary refrain from again bringing Shelley's name before the public for as long as Sir Timothy lived.[51] Mary had no choice but to agree. Considered from the viewpoint of a mother, defiance was unthinkable: far too much in her son's future depended on Sir Timothy's goodwill. Moreover, the prohibition seemed temporary enough, for, as Mary pointed out to a friend, Sir Timothy was already past seventy and could hardly live much longer.[52] Twenty years later, with Sir Timothy at last near death in his ninety-first year, Mary looked back somewhat wryly on her miscalculation.[53]

But by then, 1844, any real financial worries were at an end; and it can hardly be an accident that Mary's final publication—

Rambles in Germany and Italy—occurs in the year of Sir Timothy's
death, when Percy Florence came into the title and the inheritance.
The long struggle she had waged was finally over: her son was
Sir Percy Florence; his unambitious nature promised a most un-
Shelley-like serenity; and the income he had inherited, although
Mary might (and did) complain about its disappointing limits,
was more than sufficient for a genial young man who had no passion
at all for reforming the world.

Aside from Mary's rather ugly scare from a potential black-
mailer in 1845, some difficulties in 1845–46 with a literary forger,
the notorious "Major" Byron, and some additional difficulties
with the egregious Thomas Medwin, the remainder of her life
passed, for the most part, in an unaccustomed tranquillity that
was marred only by her failing health. She died Saturday, February 1, 1851, in her London home at 24 Chester Square, having
fallen into a coma eight days earlier.[54] Her body, at her own wish,
was buried between her mother and father—all three of them,
at Lady Shelley's instance—in St. Peter's Churchyard, Bourne-
mouth. Perhaps, if a moral may be looked for in the hard-earned
peacefulness of Mary's very last years, we can find it in the quotation
from Edmund Burke with which she ended her journal: "'Preserve
always a habit of giving.'"[55] It was an ideal that she had
attempted—however imperfectly—to fulfill during much of her
life after Shelley's death, succeeding most notably with her son;
with her aging, financially burdened, intellectually depleted father
(who died in 1836); and with the memory of the poet who had
eloped with her when she was a radiant girl of sixteen.

CHAPTER 2

Frankenstein

WHETHER or not *Frankenstein* is Mary Shelley's best novel—
and the overwhelming majority of critics seem to agree
that it is[1]—it clearly deserves a preeminent place in any study of
her career. The product of a series of coincidences and accidents,
it remains the one work by which Mary Shelley is generally known;
and, if its fame today rests in large part on the cinematic technique
and the cosmetic ingenuity of Hollywood, *Frankenstein* is nonetheless a remarkable literary achievement in its own right—"the
most wonderful work to have been written at twenty years of age
that I ever heard of," as Godwin himself declared.[2] But we need
to explore in some detail the most significant aspects of Mary
Shelley's first novel and to establish as securely as possible its
position as one of the central creative achievements of the period.
Such an effort, however, must begin with a consideration of the
devious chain of events which led to the novel's composition.

I *Claire Clairmont*

In a sense, the true origin of *Frankenstein* begins not with Mary
Shelley but with her "stepsister," Claire Clairmont, who was eight
months Mary's junior. Born April 27, 1798, Claire was not, of
course, any actual blood relative. Rather, as the second child of
Mary's stepmother, she did not enter the Godwin household until
1801, at the age of three, when Godwin and Mrs. Mary Jane Clairmont married. But, despite the extreme youth of both girls at the
time of the marriage, Claire's entrance into Mary's home must
have been a profound shock to Mary; for almost a half century
later when Mary and Claire were both well into middle age, Mary,
faced with the prospect of being left alone with Claire, suddenly
cried to her daughter-in-law who had offered to leave the room:
"Don't go, dear! don't leave me alone with her! she has been the
bane of my life ever since I was three years old!"[3]
Although it is easy enough for us to locate the probable sources

for Mary's initial, childhood resentment—Claire's unstable personality and the second Mrs. Godwin's natural preference for her own daughter—it is even easier to avoid seeing the likely cause for Claire's increasingly erratic behavior as the girls matured. Apparently, and quite humanly, a good part of the problem derived from Claire's awareness of Mary's intellectual superiority—an awareness Mary herself did little to allay. "She [that is, Mary] always thought and called [Claire] . . . stupid," the second Mrs. Godwin was to declare to a friend when both the girls were sixteen. And the reason given, one which even the partiality of a mother could not prevent Mrs. Godwin from acknowledging, was that Claire had "not such first-rate abilities as [Mary's] own."[4] Indeed, it is clear enough from a brief passage in Mary's first-published volume that she must often have treated Claire with an air of amused condescension. "On looking at this scene," Mary wrote of the elopement journey of 1814, "C*** exclaimed, 'Oh! this is beautiful enough; let us live here.' This was her exclamation on every new scene, and as each surpassed the one before, she cried, 'I am glad we did not stay [there], but let us live here.' "[5]

Nor, of course, is it likely that Shelley's marked preference for Mary before the elopement did anything but increase Claire's sense of inferiority. That she was herself strongly attracted to Shelley at the time seems certain; yet the two lovers used her, rather unfeelingly it seems, as a blind to cover their own growing intimacy from the eyes of Godwin and his wife. "Mrs. Godwin has ascertained that the two girls used to walk daily in the wilderness of the Charterhouse, where a young gentleman, who must have been Shelley, would join them. The gardener's wife says that the fair young lady [that is, Mary] always sat in one of the arbours [with Shelley], while the little young lady [Claire] would walk up and down by herself."[6] Thus Claire's decision to accompany Mary and Shelley on their elopement to the Continent has a rather pathetic aspect if we see it for what it probably was: a young girl's desire not only to share in an adventurous journey but also to participate vicariously in the love affair she had not been able to excite for herself.

Once we have established this as an inference, the obvious crisis of identity that Claire suffered during the next two or three years becomes more comprehensible. Again and again she changed her name—from "Jane" to "Clara" to "Clare" to "Claire"[7]—as if in flight from the fear of her own inner worthlessness; and it seems far more accurate to apply to her (than to Edward John Trelawny) Mary's shrewd insight into the price that association with genius can exact from the noncreative: "He is . . . destroyed by *being nothing—* destroyed by envy and internal dissatisfaction."[8]

For surely it is not a sentimentalization to say that Claire was destroyed by her need to live at the level of genius, without having the necessary qualifications. In art, she could not escape the pressure of comparison; for she complained to a friend, when in her thirties, that "in our family, if you cannot write an epic poem or novel that by its originality knocks all other novels on the head, you are a despicable creature, not worth acknowledging."[9] But despite this pressure and the undoubted vivacity of her letters, Claire herself was sadly unable to achieve anything more than the shadow of a successful literary creation. In 1814, to concentrate only upon the efforts of her earlier years, she attempted a novel ("The Ideot") while Mary was beginning "Hate." In 1816, she was again competing, if indirectly, with Mary's *Frankenstein.* In 1817, a now lost novel of hers met only with rejection from publishers.

Granted her personality, then, it is not surprising to find Claire turning to the obvious, vicarious alternative: intimate association with a creative personality. Her first attempt was to draw Shelley away from Mary, evidently seizing as her opportunity Mary's ill-health and advanced pregnancy in the autumn and winter of 1814–15. Then, after Claire had succeeded so well that Mary was compelled to insist on her departure from the household,[10] Claire threw herself, early in the following year, into a disastrous liaison with the most famous poet of the age, Lord Byron.

The general consequences of that liaison are, of course, well known. In early 1817, Claire bore Byron a daughter; in 1818, at Byron's insistence, the child was placed in his care alone; by 1820, Claire's earlier excessive infatuation for her lover had turned into an equally exaggerated hatred; and, in 1822, the child died, partly due to Byron's neglect, leaving Claire another half century and more (she died in 1879) to brood with pathological intensity about her demon lover. Not so well known, however—or at least not so determinate in its specific details—is the question of the more immediate consequences of the liaison. Indeed, there are problems pertinent enough to justify a brief look at them.

II *Byron and the Road to Geneva*

Byron's marriage had already disintegrated when Claire began
throwing herself desperately and persistently in his path in 1816.
Several of her early letters to him survive,[11] and from them we
can hardly avoid seeing that Claire's own neurotic needs engineered
what followed. She offered herself to him quite openly, insisted
that marriage was something she despised, and succeeded at last
in becoming his mistress. Unhappily for Claire, once her desire had
been achieved, there was no easy going back for her either physically
or emotionally. By the time Byron set sail for the Continent on
April 25, she was pregnant; and her emotional involvement was
such that she was willing to travel alone to Geneva for a rendezvous,
an offer which quite appalled Byron.[12] But, if Byron proved far
less tractable than Claire had hoped, Shelley was another matter.
He and Mary for some time had dreamed of an "Italian scheme"—
of departing from the hostile climate of England and of beginning
a more pleasant life in Italy.[13] On May 3, 1816, however, he,
Mary, and Claire departed with precipitate suddenness, not for
Italy, but for Switzerland.[14] Under Shelley's ostensible protection,
Claire was to have her rendezvous in Geneva after all.

Exactly what role Mary herself played in inducing Shelley to
travel to Geneva is a complex question—but it is not an idle one;
for the personality of Byron was to exert a seminal influence not
only on *Frankenstein* but on Mary's subsequent novels.[15] The
following details, at any rate, seem certain: through Claire, Mary
met Byron shortly before his departure from England; she was
enormously impressed by him; she eagerly anticipated seeing him
again; and Claire accommodatingly suggested to Byron that
Mary would "no doubt" become his mistress when they met once
more at Geneva.[16]

That Mary did not become Byron's mistress is evident. Not so
evident, however, is her part in the decision which had such a
profound effect on her own career, on Shelley's, and on Byron's.
The question, in fact, is whether or not Mary was as instrumental
as Claire in persuading Shelley to go to Geneva. Claire, we know,
wrote to Byron to say that Shelley had "yielded to my pressing
solicitations" to undertake the journey.[17] Yet, as we also know,
in the preceding year Mary had fought bitterly against Claire's

influence on Shelley; and she had succeeded so well that Claire was compelled for a time to live in another part of England.[18] It seems obvious, then, that Mary was—at the least—a tacit partner in Claire's "solicitations." More than this, granted the prompt and radical nature of Shelley's decision—for he left England less than two weeks after Byron—the conclusion follows that Mary was much more than a merely tacit partner of Claire's. After all, Byron was an extraordinarily fascinating man, and he appears to have turned Mary's head for the moment almost as intoxicatingly as he had Claire's. "Mary is delighted with you," Claire wrote to her lover after the three had met together in London, "as I knew she would be; she entreats me in private to obtain your address abroad that we may, if possible, have again the pleasure of seeing you. She perpetually exclaims: 'How mild he is! How gentle! How different from what I expected.' "[19]

III *The Origin of* Frankenstein

Shelley, Mary, and Claire reached the outskirts of Geneva on May 13, 1816, taking lodgings at a hotel one mile outside the city. But, although Byron had left England more than a week earlier, his more leisurely rate of travel—as well as the illness of his paid traveling companion, the eccentric Dr. John William Polidori— retarded his progress to such a degree that he did not arrive at Geneva until almost two weeks after them. Nor did his tardiness belie his feelings about Claire. At least four times she wrote to him within the next two days of his arrival, her notes increasingly concerned at his failure to respond.[20] Indeed, whether even her last, most importunate note to him would have produced the desired result is an open question—one, happily, which it is un- necessary to answer. For between Claire's fourth note (written sometime after two in the morning) and the rendezvous it sug- gested in her room (at 7:30 that same evening), Byron, returning from an expedition of house-hunting, met Shelley for the first time on May 27, on the shores of Lake Geneva.[21]

The friendship which swiftly developed between the two poets is, of course, justly regarded as one of the most significant in English literary history. Although the details of it have been told too often to need rehearsing here, the following account of the attraction that flared between the two (as described in Thomas Moore's early biography of Byron) is of interest because it clearly draws upon Mary Shelley's own version of the friendship:

> The conversation of Mr. Shelley, from the extent of his poetic reading, and the strange mystic speculations into which his system of philosophy let him, was of a nature strongly to arrest and interest the attention of Lord Byron, and to turn him away from worldly associations and topics into more abstract and untrodden ways of thought. As far as contrast, indeed, is an enlivening ingredient of such intercourse, it would be difficult to find two persons more formed to whet each other's faculties by discussion, as on few points of common interest between them did their opinions agree; and that this difference had its root deep in the conformation of their respective minds needs but a glance through the rich glittering labyrinth of Mr. Shelley's pages to assure us. [22]

Even more interesting is that this very tendency of Shelley and Byron "to whet each other's faculties by discussion" led to the origin of *Frankenstein*—at least according to Mary. But whether she was exaggerating Byron's importance or not, the general significance of his presence is clear. Because both parties soon became dissatisfied with the hotel where they were staying, they occupied by early June separate houses on the south shore of Lake Geneva— Shelley, Mary, and Claire residing at the Maison Chappuis;[23] Byron and Polidori settling a short walk away at the Villa Diodati. At first, with the weather holding fair, much of their time was passed together in boating on the lake. "But," as Mary tells us, "it proved a wet, ungenial summer, and incessant rain often confined us for days to the house."[24] Under such circumscribed conditions, the larger dimensions of the Villa Diodati became the natural social center for both parties; and, as Mary described those wet evenings to Byron's biographer, "we often sat up in conversation till the morning light. There was never any lack of subjects, and, grave or gay, we were always interested."[25]

During one of these evenings of talk, the topic turned to composition as a means of passing the time. Both parties had been reading a collection of German ghost stories translated into French by one Jean Baptiste Benoît Eyriès—the *Fantasmagoriana, ou Recueil d'Histoires d'Apparitions....*[26] It remained for Byron to suggest that each of them attempt a ghost story of his own. "You and I," he added to Mary, "will publish ours together."[27] Unhappily, at this point something of a conflict arises between Mary's account of the novel's genesis and other, independent pieces of evidence. According to Mary, "there were four of us" in the friendly competition. Actually, of course, there were five, including Claire.[28] Mary then describes herself as being caught in a painful, non-productive impasse:

I busied myself *to think of a story*—a story to rival those which had excited us to this task. One which would speak to the mysterious fears of our nature and awaken thrilling horror—one to make the reader dread to look round, to curdle the blood, and quicken the beatings of the heart. If I did not accomplish these things, my ghost story would be unworthy of its name. I thought and pondered—vainly. I felt that blank incapability of invention which is the greatest misery of authorship when dull Nothing replies to our anxious invocations. "Have you thought of a story?" I was asked each morning, and each morning I was forced to reply with a mortifying negative. (Author's Introduction, 1831)

The difficulty of accepting this account of a long struggle of gestation is that Polidori, in his diary entry for June 17 (only a day or two after the competition had started), complained of his own, singular inactivity: "The ghost-stories are begun by all but me."[29] Furthermore, Mary's version of how her impasse was finally overcome may reflect her own (half-conscious) fascination for Byron rather than the actual situation at Diodati in 1816:

Many and long were the conversations between Lord Byron and Shelley to which I was a devout but nearly silent listener. During one of these, various philosophical doctrines were discussed, and among others the nature of the principle of life, and whether there was any probability of its ever being discovered and communicated. They talked of the experiments of Dr. Darwin . . . who preserved a piece of vermicelli in a glass case till by some extraordinary means it began to move with voluntary motion. Not thus, after all, would life be given. Perhaps a corpse would be reanimated; galvanism had given token of such things: perhaps the component parts of a creature might be manufactured, brought together, and endued with vital warmth. (Author's Introduction, 1831)

This hint, according to Mary, so possessed her imagination that, a few hours afterward, as she lay in bed, a series of images began to pass through her mind: "I saw the pale student of unhallowed arts kneeling beside the thing he had put together. I saw the hideous phantasm of a man stretched out, and then, on the working of some powerful engine, show signs of life, and stir with an uneasy, half-vital motion. . . . On the morrow I announced that I had thought of a story."

But the question arises as to whether it was indeed with Byron that Shelley had the talk which so aroused Mary's imagination. On June 15, Polidori wrote in his diary that "Shelley and I had a conversation about principles—whether man was to be thought merely an instrument."[30] Because of this clue and because of the fact that Polidori was an unusually knowledgeable physician in areas which would touch upon the question of reanimation, it has recently been suggested that Mary was in error; that the conversation of June 15 between Shelley and Polidori (*not* Byron) was what actually first sparked her imagination; that on June 16 Byron's suggestion that they all attempt a ghost story followed; and that by June 17 Mary, as Polidori's diary for that date seems to indicate, had already begun writing.[31]

Despite the often convincing consistency of this argument, however, a number of difficulties persist. For one thing, of course, there is Mary's own word. In fact, nine years before she sat down to describe the composition of *Frankenstein,* Mary alluded in her journal to the nightly conversations at Diodati, "entirely tête-à-tête" between Shelley and Byron.[32] For another, Polidori's own laconic description of the conversation of June 15—"whether man was to be thought merely an instrument"—sounds rather more like a discussion of determinism than of reanimation. For still another reason, it seems undeniable that a mind so preternaturally alert as Byron's could easily have picked up a good deal of superficial knowledge from the garrulous Polidori and given it back to Shelley in the course of a friendly discussion. Last of all, and perhaps restoring something of Mary's reputation for accuracy at the expense of Polidori's, Shelley wrote to Mary in 1818 praising her for what she had produced at Geneva during his absence—a reference, it would seem, to Mary's beginning *Frankenstein* in earnest sometime between June 23 and June 30, 1816, at least one week after Byron's initial suggestion.[33] At any rate, we can sum up the question by conceding that Mary's account of the origin of *Frankenstein* is far from watertight but that, aside from our being alert to a quite possible exaggeration of Byron's importance, it must remain our chief guide to the details of how the novel came to be written.

IV *Composition*

It is also interesting to note that in Mary's account of the origins of *Frankenstein* she tells us that she began with what is now (in the 1831 edition) Chapter 5: "It was on a dreary night of November. . . ." If this statement is correct, however, we are confronted at once with an obvious difficulty. For Chapter 5 in the 1831 edition was only the fourth chapter in the novel when it was first published;[34] and Mary wrote to Shelley in December, 1816, almost a half year after she had begun composition, that she had just completed Chapter 4.[35] In other words, to reconcile Mary's statement in the 1831 introduction with other indications of how the novel was composed, we must posit something like the following: First, Mary began a short tale in June, 1816, beginning with the words, "It was a dreary night in November. . . ." She then decided, either in July or August, to expand what she had already written into a larger work. By December, 1816, expansion and revision had carried her to the end of what is now Chapter 5, the creation of the monster, leaving her presumably with a body of yet unrevised material (perhaps including something of the monster's narrative) to be worked into the context of the expanded scheme.[36]

At any rate, this last point—the existence of an undetermined amount of original material carrying the story *past* the creation of the monster—seems to be supported by the probabilities of arithmetic. In December, 1816, as we have seen, Mary announced completion of the fourth chapter (Chapter 5 in the 1831 edition). Yet the novel was finished by May of the following year, despite a series of interruptions extending from mid-December to late February; and the novel contained, when published in 1818, a total of twenty-three chapters (twenty-four in the 1831 edition). Thus, it seems reasonable to assume that this much faster rate of composition after the completion of the chapter describing the monster's creation was due to the existence of a core story in some degree of rough draft.

Nor, of course, would such an indirect pattern of composition be at all unusual. As we know from many a Henry James and Joseph Conrad preface, it is not uncommon for the novelist to begin with what is essentially an anecdotal nucleus and then to work from it in his imagination, backward and forward, elaborating both the causes and the consequences of the dramatic situation which first aroused his interest. Furthermore, Mary had a specific motive for expanding upon her original opening. As she herself relates in the 1831 introduction, "At first I thought but of a few pages, of a short tale, but Shelley urged me to develop the idea at greater length."

Indeed, much of the material preceding the "germ" idea of the novel (that is, letters 1–4 from Walton to his sister, as well as chapters 1–4 of Frankenstein's narrative) was seemingly not composed until the latter part of 1816, along with the revision of what is now Chapter 5. We can assume this with some confidence from the evidence of Mary's journal. Because the journal for the period May 14, 1815–July 20, 1816 has been lost, the first extant entry dealing with *Frankenstein* occurs on July 24, 1816. There Mary simply remarks: "I . . . write my story."[37] On August 21, after devoting what appears to be four weeks of reasonably steady work on *Frankenstein,* Mary notes that "Shelley and I talk about my story."[38] (Quite possibly, it was in this conference that Shelley suggested expansion, not only generally, but specifically as well; for he was reading Milton on this date [see below, sections VII and VIII].)

On August 29, a little over a week after this conference, the Shelleys and the now noticeably pregnant Claire left Geneva for England. There, living at Bath with Claire, Mary soon began to reread parts of Richardson's *Clarissa;* and, within the next two months, read as well and for the first time both of Richardson's other novels, *Pamela* and *Sir Charles Grandison.*[39] Since the prologue to *Frankenstein* consists of four letters written by Walton to his sister, the fourth of which is actually a journal in the Richardsonian manner (as is, indeed, the novel's conclusion), it is tempting to believe—and I suggest reasonable to conclude—that Mary's interest in the epistolary novel at this time was closely related to the portions of the novel she herself was then writing.

Following the completion of Chapter 4 on December 5, however, several events occurred which apparently made work on the novel intermittent for some time afterward. On December 10, Harriet Shelley's body was found in the Serpentine River in Hyde Park; on December 30, Shelley, now legally free, married Mary in London; on January 12, 1817, Claire gave birth to Byron's daughter, Clara Allegra; and on January 24, the trial began in Chancery to determine whether Shelley and Mary were fit parents for Harriet's now motherless children.

But despite so many distractions, Mary was at work on the novel either by late February or early March; and she steadily wrote each day, until by April 9, the first draft was finished.[40] A period of revision then followed. From April 10 to April 17, Mary made the same entry in her journal: "Correct *Frankenstein*."[41] On April 18, the tedious labor of transcription began and continued until May 13; then, on the following day, May 14, 1817, Mary wrote in her journal with what we must assume was a note of mingled triumph and relief: "Finis."[42]

V *Publication and Initial Reception*

The labor of composition ended, the task of finding a publisher began, a task that was to prove somewhat more difficult than Mary had apparently first thought. In the latter part of May, she traveled to London with the manuscript and submitted it to John Murray, entering in her journal the promising comment that the publisher liked it.[43] Unfortunately, William Gifford, the editor of the *Quarterly Review* and one of Murray's literary advisers, gave a negative verdict, no doubt in part because he regarded the book as too radical in its social and political implications.[44] Charles Ollier, Shelley's own publisher, was tried next, in early August.[45] Again the manuscript was rejected, apparently with insulting promptness.[46] Finally, in late August, still another publisher, Lackington's, expressed interest; and, with Shelley handling most of the details, the novel was accepted the following month, receiving publication six months later, on March 11, 1818.[47]

The book was widely noticed. As might be expected, the *Quarterly Review* (whose editor, as we have seen, advised Murray against publication) was for the most part unfavorable. Although the reviewer granted some praise to the "highly terrific" language and to the "rationality" of the preface (an unwittingly amusing touch since Shelley, and not Mary, had written the 1817 preface), he complained that "our taste and our judgment alike revolt at this kind of writing, and the greater the ability with which it may be executed, the worse it is—it inculcates no lesson of conduct, manners, or morality; it cannot mend, and will not even amuse its readers, unless their taste have been deplorably vitiated."[48] The

Edinburgh Magazine, rather more generous in its review, spoke of
the book's "power of fascination" and of its "mastery in harsh and
savage delineations of passion"; but the reviewer agreed with the
Quarterly in his remark that "it is one of those works . . . which,
when we have read, we do not well see why it should have been
written."[49]

It was Sir Walter Scott (to whom Shelley had sent a copy of
the novel in January)[50] who gave the book its warmest praise
in a review published in *Blackwood's*:

[In] this extraordinary tale . . . the author seems to us to disclose uncommon powers of poetic imagination. The feeling with which we perused
the unexpected and fearful, yet, allowing the possibility of the event, very
natural conclusion of Frankenstein's experiment, shook a little even our
firm nerves. . . .

It is no slight merit in our eyes, that the tale, though wild in incident, is
written in plain and forcible English. . . . The ideas of the author are
always clearly as well as forcibly expressed; and his descriptions of land-
scape have in them the choice requisites of truth, freshness, precision, and
beauty. . . .

[Improbability might be found in] the self-education of the monster, considering the slender opportunities of acquiring knowledge that he possessed. . . . We should also be disposed . . . to question whether the monster,
how tall, agile and strong however, could have perpetrated so much mischief
undiscovered. . . .

But . . . upon the whole, the work impresses us with a high idea of the
author's original genius and happy power of expression. We . . . congratu-
late our readers upon a novel which excites new reflections and untried
sources of emotion.[51]

With such widespread attention, coupled with the book's intrinsic merit, it is hardly surprising that *Frankenstein* became one
of the literary events of 1818. "I passed a day or two with St. Croix
and his bride this last week," Thomas Love Peacock wrote to
Shelley in late August. "I went to the Egham races. I met on the
course a great number of my old acquaintance, by the reading
portion of whom I was asked a multitude of questions concerning
Frankenstein and its author. It seems to be universally known and
read. The criticism of the *Quarterly,* though unfriendly, contained
many admissions of its merit, and must on the whole have done
it service."[52]

VI *The Novel*

Structurally, *Frankenstein* reflects Mary's full involvement in what we sometimes naively regard as a "modern" technical concern for the novelist—the question of point of view. Indeed, the novel can be accurately described as a construct of three separate narrators, each representing a different point of view—Robert Walton, the would-be Arctic explorer, who is the voice of both prologue and epilogue; Victor Frankenstein, the creator of the monster, who ostensibly narrates the twenty-four chapters; and the monster himself, who is the true speaking voice of the near-mathematical center of the book, chapters 11–16. In this respect, then, *Frankenstein* bears a highly interesting similarity to that astonishing creation of another female novelist—Emily Brontë's *Wuthering Heights,* published thirty years afterward. And however greater we may assess Emily Brontë's success in the manipulation of her narrative voices, the similarity of the technique in the two novels indicates a common artistic strategy: the use of an initial narrator, himself a nonparticipant in the central action, who leads the reader by a series of more or less "natural" steps onto (and across) the outskirts of an unnatural world.

But "point of view" also contributes inevitably to meaning, and we can find in the contrast and interplay among the three narrators a valuable index to one of the most prominent themes of the novel: the ambiguous nature of ambition and its potentially dehumanizing effect even on those with the most generous intentions. The opening paragraphs of *Frankenstein* sound this note of ambition unmistakably. Walton has traveled from England to St. Petersburg for the purpose of carrying out an "undertaking" to which he is willing to devote his entire life. His ostensible goal, we quickly learn, is one of exploration. By sailing northward into uncharted regions, he will at last arrive where "snow and frost are banished" in "a land surpassing in wonders and in beauty every region hitherto discovered on the habitable globe." But even if the existence of this undiscovered continent prove illusory—Walton continues in his first letter to his sister—"you cannot contest the inestimable benefit which I shall confer on all mankind, to the last generation, by discovering a passage near the pole to those countries, to reach which at present so many months are requisite."

At first glance, such a high-minded purpose, with its expressed wish of benefiting "all mankind," seems exemplary. When we look more closely at Walton's opening letter, however, we see that his actual goal is nothing more or less than personal "glory." His current dream of eminence as a great explorer is only the outcome of the failure of an earlier fantasy: the vision of himself as a great poet "in the temple where the names of Homer and Shakespeare are consecrated." In short, there is a paradoxical split within Walton, and it radiates from the very nature of his ambition. On the one hand, as we have seen, he hopes to benefit "all mankind"; on the other, he desires to raise himself to an eminence which will make him unique—that is, which will assure him, by his personal prominence, that he is quite different from "all mankind." And we can see this second wish revealingly expressed in the image he holds of himself as explorer: "I shall satiate my ardent curiosity with the sight of the world never before visited, and may tread a land never before imprinted by the foot of man."

Consequently, the concomitant of Walton's intense ambition is a painful sense of isolation. "I have no friend, Margaret," he complains in his second letter. "You may deem me romantic, my dear sister, but I bitterly feel the want of a friend. I have no one near me . . . whose tastes are like my own, to approve or amend my plans. How would such a friend repair the faults of your poor brother! . . . I greatly need a friend who would have sense enough not to despise me as romantic, and affection enough for me to endeavour to regulate my mind." Indeed, even the nature of Walton's goal—his voyaging farther and farther into a world of ice—is a fitting metaphor for the emotional cost of his ambition.[53] And when, in his fourth letter, Walton describes his first encounter with Victor Frankenstein, we are given a powerful concretion, in dramatic and visual terms, of the ultimate price intense ambition exacts from the psyche:

Last Monday (July 31st) we were nearly surrounded by ice, which closed in the ship on all sides, scarcely leaving her the sea-room in which she floated. . . . About two hours after . . . we heard the ground sea, and before night the ice broke and freed our ship. . . . In the morning, however, as soon as it was light, I went upon deck and found all the sailors busy on one side of the vessel, apparently talking to someone in the sea. It was, in fact, a sledge . . . which had drifted towards us in the night on a large fragment of ice. Only one dog remained alive; but there was a human being within it whom the sailors were persuading to enter the vessel. . . .

On perceiving me, the stranger addressed me in English, although with a foreign accent. "Before I come on board your vessel," said he, "will you have the kindness to inform me whither you are bound?"

For the question Frankenstein asks from the ice is the logical outcome of his own ambition. Alone now, "nearly frozen," his closest human relationships severed by the monster (whom Frankenstein himself has created), "his body dreadfully emaciated by fatigue and suffering," Frankenstein yet posits as a condition of his renewing human contact that Walton and his crew continue in the same direction as he. In other words, the initial confrontation between Walton and Frankenstein throws into sudden high relief the sense of isolation Walton himself has been brooding on, along with Walton's fierce desire to drive on to an intellectually predetermined goal.

And this visual and dramatically rendered verdict on the cost of intense ambition is reinforced in didactic fashion by Frankenstein himself in one of the first conversations between the two men. "Unhappy man!" he cries to Walton when the latter has revealed his hope for achievement. "Do you share my madness? Have you drunk also of the intoxicating draught? Hear me; let me reveal my tale, and you will dash the cup from your lips!"[54] Later, his "tale" well under way, Frankenstein reemphasizes his didactic intention: "I see by your eagerness and the wonder and hope which your eyes express, my friend, that you expect to be informed of the secret with which I am acquainted; that cannot be; listen patiently until the end of my story, and you will easily perceive why I am reserved upon that subject. . . . Learn from me, if not by my precepts, at least by my example, how dangerous is the acquirement of knowledge and how much happier that man is who believes his native town to be the world, than he who aspires to become greater than this nature will allow" (Chapter 4).

On one level, then, the twenty-four chapters of Frankenstein's narrative can be taken as an extended homily on the dangers of ambition.[55] For it is clear that the "point of view" expressed by Frankenstein is a broad and increasingly deepening variation on Walton's own Faustian vision. "It was the secrets of heaven and earth that I desired to learn," Frankenstein tells Walton in a description of his early hopes; "and whether it was the outward substance of things or the inner spirit of nature and the mysterious soul

of man that occupied me, still my inquiries were directed to the
metaphysical, or in its highest sense, the physical secrets of the
world" (Chapter 2). And soon afterward, in an image of exploration remarkably akin to Walton's own dream of glory,
Frankenstein describes how his ambitions received new life and
force during a lecture on the history of science at the University
of Ingolstadt: "So much has been done, exclaimed the soul of
Frankenstein—more, far more, will I achieve; treading in the steps
already marked, I will pioneer a new way, explore unknown powers,
and unfold to the world the deepest mysteries of creation" (Chapter 3).

Thus, the over-all import of Frankenstein's tale—its tripartite
structure of fierce ambition, unparalleled achievement, and fright-
ful personal cost—provides a paradigm for Walton powerful enough
to transform (at least temporarily) his system of values. Like the
Wedding Guest at the end of the Ancient Mariner's tale of Coleridge,
Walton undergoes a moral transformation due to the intense
nature of what he has heard. And, in a sharp revulsion from his
earlier dreams, he writes to his sister: "It is terrible to reflect that
the lives of all these men [that is, the crew he has hired] are en-
dangered through me. If we are lost, my mad schemes are the
cause."[56]

Indeed, it is clear that this reading is sustained by the nature of
the monster himself. For the monster is quite literally the embodiment of Frankenstein's ambition, and it is that embodiment
which slays, in turn, each of Frankenstein's dearest human attachments—first little William, his brother; then Justine Moritz,
an especial favorite of his; then Henry Clerval, his best friend;
then Elizabeth, his bride; and finally, indirectly, his father. There
is even, in a sudden access of dread on Frankenstein's part after
the death of Elizabeth, a moment of insight for him in which he
sees that nothing at all of human relationship will be left to him by
the ultimate effects of his ambition—as, in truth, nothing is left
when Walton meets him on the fragment of ice:

> After an interval I arose, and as if by instinct, crawled into the room where
> the corpse of my beloved lay. There were women weeping around; I hung
> over it and joined my sad tears to theirs; all this time no distinct idea
> presented itself to my mind, but my thoughts rambled to various sub-
> jects, reflecting confusedly on my misfortunes and their cause. I was
> bewildered, in a cloud of wonder and horror. The death of William, the

execution of Justine, the murder of Clerval, and lastly of my wife; even at that moment I knew not that my only remaining friends were safe from the malignity of the fiend; my father even now might be writhing under his grasp, and Ernest [Frankenstein's surviving brother] might be dead at his feet. (Chapter 23)

And so Frankenstein's obsessive pursuit of the monster to wreak vengeance on him (a pursuit which begins and ends in Chapter 24) is doomed to failure. He can hardly be expected to capture that which is an aspect of himself,[57] and his chase can have no other result but his own death.

But in the content of the novel's third "point of view"—the monster's own narrative—we find the most subtle variation on the theme of ambition. For the monster, inhuman himself, feels as his deepest need the desire for a human relationship. "But where were my friends and relations?" he asks rhetorically of Frankenstein. "No father had watched my infant days, no mother had blessed me with smiles and caresses; or if they had, all my past life was now a blot, a blind vacancy in which I distinguished nothing. From my earliest remembrance I had been as I then was in height and proportion. I had never yet seen a being resembling me or who claimed any intercourse with me" (Chapter 13). And he concludes his narrative by demanding that Frankenstein create a mate for him: "We may not part until you have promised to comply with my requisition. I am alone and miserable; man will not associate with me; but one as deformed and horrible as myself would not deny herself to me. My companion must be of the same species and have the same defects. This being you must create. . . . You must create a female for me with whom I can live in the interchange of those sympathies necessary for my being" (Chapters 16, 17).

In short, in a successful fusion of image and idea, Mary has endowed the embodiment of Frankenstein's ambition with a speaking voice that pleads most urgently for the presence of the very thing Frankenstein's (and Walton's) dream of glory has rejected—genuine human companionship. That voice of the monster's, then—isolated, pleading, unceasingly conscious of its desperate loneliness—takes on a much greater resonance when we hear it for what it logically is: the submerged cry for fellowship at the heart of an intense ambition. And, as we have seen with Walton, the paradoxical nature of ambition (even of an ambition

most benevolent in its intention) dooms that cry to disappointment.
Intense ambition can be experienced only by a sensibility which
has envisioned itself as distinct from ordinary humanity; and the
sense of loneliness persists because it must—the inevitable psychological price for the dream of glorious achievement. It is one mark
of the brilliance of Mary Shelley's conception—however flawed
and clumsy the individual sections of her novel may be[58]—that
at the heart of *Frankenstein* is a persistent, undeniably moving
cry for fellowship and that the cry is encased in a monstrous form
doomed to assert repeatedly the murderous autonomy of excessive
ambition.

VII *Victor Frankenstein's Dual Role*

But the implications of *Frankenstein* can be seen to cut much
more deeply than would a mere expatiation upon the wisdom of
Pope's couplet of a century earlier: *"Know thy own point: This
kind, this due degree/Of blindness, weakness, Heaven bestows on
thee."* (Essay on Man, I, 283—84). Indeed, it is quite clear that
Frankenstein, like Shelley's *Alastor* (1816), reflects a most ambiguous attitude toward the conflict between the individual desire
for fulfillment and the persistent social demand for the compromise
of individuality necessary in human relationships.

Thus in Shelley's poem, both subtitle *(The Spirit of Solitude)*
and preface seem to promise the reader a reassuring poetic homily—
in the best eighteenth-century tradition—on the sturdy superiority
of social virtues. "The picture [given in the poem of the central
figure's disappointment and death] is not barren of instruction
to actual men," Shelley writes in the preface. "The Poet's self-
centred seclusion was avenged by the furies [the avenging spirit
of solitude] of an irresistible passion pursuing him to speedy
ruin. . . . Among those who attempt to exist without human sympathy, the pure and tender-hearted perish through the intensity
and passion of their search after its communities, when the vacancy
of their spirit suddenly makes itself felt." Yet, in the poem itself,
the reassuring social moral dissolves under the glorification of the
dead Poet who rejected all but his own, personal dream:

> *Art and eloquence,*
> *And all the shows o' the world are frail and vain*
> *To weep a loss that turns their lights to shade.*

It is a woe "too deep for tears," when all
Is reft at once, when some surpassing Spirit,
Whose light adorned the world around it, leaves
Those who remain behind, not sobs or groans,
The passionate tumult of a clinging hope;
But pale despair and cold tranquillity.

(*Alastor*, 710–18)

And so it is in *Frankenstein*, where the ostensible didactic surface is undercut by quite contradictory implications. For, if we can argue that the over-all effect of Frankenstein's "tale" upon Walton is to cause the would-be explorer, however reluctantly, to view his earlier dreams of glory as "mad," it is equally certain that in the heart of Frankenstein, even as he dies, burns an unrepentant flame of hope: "Farewell, Walton! Seek happiness in tranquillity and avoid ambition, even if it be only the apparently innocent one of distinguishing yourself in science and discoveries. Yet why do I say this? I have myself been blasted in these hopes, yet another may succeed."[59] And the persistence of this dream, even in the face of the most painful disillusionment, suggests a secondary, subversive theme: that in the very nature of man, under the present conditions of spiritual and social oppression, a radical split resides, condemning him to a perpetual sense of nonfulfillment.

When we recognize this aspect of the novel, the uneasiness of the first reviewers becomes more understandable. The review article in the *Edinburgh Review*, for example, spoke of "views ... bordering too closely on impiety," and then complained that, although a sound moral (that is, one congenial to the conservative spirit of Pope's couplet) might be found in *Frankenstein*, the author had gone much too far in the audacity of his imagination: "Some of our highest and most reverential feelings receive a shock from the conception on which [the book] turns, so as to produce a painful and bewildered state of mind while we peruse it.... It might, indeed, be the author's view to shew that the powers of man have been wisely limited, and that misery would follow their extension,—but still the expression, 'Creator', applied to a mere human being, gives us [a sensation] of shock.[60]

Nor, of course, was this sensation of "shock" anything but an intended effect on Mary's part. The subtitle to *Frankenstein* is

The Modern Prometheus; and the novel's epigraph is taken from
Paradise Lost (X. 743–45): *"Did I request thee, Maker, from my
clay,/To mould me Man, did I solicit thee/From darkness to promote
me?"* That is, the unmistakable implication of both together is
to cast Victor Frankenstein in a dual role. On the one hand, he
is that Promethean figure striving against human limitations to
bring more light and benefit to mankind—a sort of prose Shelley,
as it were, at least in the early stages of his career. On the other
hand, as the novel proceeds and Frankenstein carries out the
traditional achievement of Prometheus by forming and giving
life to man, he clearly transcends his merely Promethean aspect
and becomes, in the texture of the novel, a version of the "Creator"—
of God Himself. And in this second role—especially in the relationship between Frankenstein and his creature—we find a pervasive
criticism of orthodox piety.

"All men hate the wretched," the monster declares to Frankenstein; "how, then, must I be hated, who am miserable beyond
all living things! Yet you, my creator, detest and spurn me, thy
creature" (Chapter 10). Still later, as the monster recalls the anguish
he has endured because the life given him has fallen so short of his
innate desires, he cries bitterly to Frankenstein: "Cursed, cursed
creator! Why did I live? Why . . . did I not extinguish the spark
of existence which you had so wantonly bestowed?" (Chapter 16).
In other words, what Mary Shelley is clearly doing, through the
monster, is asserting one fundamental ground for denying the
concept of a benevolent deity. Since man is so undeniably limited
under the present order of things—so frequently oppressed by his
sense of incompleteness—then his existence, at least as the orthodox
conceive it, must be regarded more as a curse than as a blessing.

And this suggestion that the present ruling power of the world
falls short of benevolence is expanded into an implication of actual
tyranny through the fusion in the monster of the two central Chris-
tian symbols of the loss of divine favor—Satan and Adam. "Oh,
Frankenstein," the monster pleads, "be not equitable to every
other and trample upon me alone, to whom thy justice, and even
thy clemency and affection, is most due. Remember that I am thy
creature; I ought to be thy Adam, but I am rather the fallen angel,
whom thou drivest from joy for no misdeed" (Chapter 10). Again,
in his account of the effect the reading of *Paradise Lost* has had
upon him, the monster, by his ignorance of the true condition of

fallen Adam, suggests once more the theme of divine oppression:

> But *Paradise Lost* excited different and far deeper emotions. I read it,
> as I had read the other volumes which had fallen into my hands, as a true
> history. It moved every feeling of wonder and awe that the picture of an
> omnipotent God warring with his creatures was capable of exciting. I often
> referred the several situations, as their similarity struck me, to my own.
> Like Adam, I was apparently united by no link to any other being in exis-
> tence; but his state was far different from mine in every other respect.
> He had come forth from the hands of God a perfect creature, happy and
> prosperous, guarded by the especial care of his Creator; he was allowed to
> converse with and acquire knowledge from beings of a superior nature, but I
> was wretched, helpless, and alone. Many times I considered Satan as the
> fitter emblem of my condition, for often, like him, when I viewed the bliss
> of my protectors [the family he is living near], the bitter gall of envy rose
> within me. (Chapter 15)

For, if the monster looks upon Adam's condition as preferable
to Satan's, Victor Frankenstein is himself corrective to that illusion.
As a composite of "Modern Prometheus," fallen Adam, and
enchained Satan, Frankenstein asserts an identity among all three,
as well as pointing to the disintegrative sense of incompleteness
that is man's fate under the orthodox deity. "Sweet and beloved
Elizabeth!" Frankenstein says to Walton, likening himself to
Adam as he recalls the period leading to his marriage. "I read and
reread her letter, and some softened feelings stole into my heart
and dared to whisper paradisiacal dreams of love and joy; but the
apple was already eaten, and the angel's arm bared to drive me
from all hope" (Chapter 22). And later, as Frankenstein draws
near to death, he points to the similarity between his destiny and
that of Prometheus and Satan:

> My feelings are profound, but I possessed a coolness of judgment that
> fitted me for illustrious achievements. This sentiment of the worth of my
> nature supported me while others would have been oppressed, for I deemed
> it criminal to throw away in useless grief those talents that might be useful
> to my fellow creatures. When I reflected on the work I had completed,
> no less a one than the creation of a sensitive and rational animal, I could
> not rank myself with the herd of common projectors. But this thought,
> which supported me in the commencement of my career, now serves only
> to plunge me lower in the dust. All my speculations and hopes are as noth-

ing, and like the archangel who aspired to omnipotence, I am chained in an eternal hell.[61]

In this respect, then, in the novel's presentation of Victor Frankenstein as a "Modern Prometheus" condemned to suffer guilt and isolation for the grandeur of his aspirations, *Frankenstein* comes remarkably close to the theme of Byron's own "Prometheus," written in the summer of 1816 while Mary was working on the earlier stages of her book. "Titan!" Byron apostrophizes,

> to thee the strife was given
> Between the suffering and the will,
> Which torture where they cannot kill:
> And the inexorable Heaven,
> And the deaf tyranny of Fate,
> The ruling principle of Hate,
> Which for its pleasure doth create
> The things it may annihilate.
> .   .   .
> Like thee, man is in part divine,
> A troubled stream from a pure source;
> And man in portions can foresee
> His own funereal destiny;
> His wretchedness and his resistance,
> And his sad unallied existence.

And this similarity between poem and novel takes on unusual significance when we realize how much light it sheds on a relatively neglected question: the interrelationship and interinfluence among three people that summer—Shelley, Byron, and Mary. For Byron, as we know, produced his "Prometheus" as the direct result of Shelley's translation of Aeschylus' drama;[62] Shelley, in his turn, if we are to believe the Byron scholars,[63] drew from this contact with Byron the original impetus for what was to culminate in his masterpiece, *Prometheus Unbound* (1818–19). But what no one seems to have recognized, at least so far as I have been able to discover, is that Mary's novel provides in many places a transitional point between the Byronic view of Prometheus (as evidenced in his short poem) and the Shelleyan transformation of the Titan in *Prometheus Unbound*.[64]

Thus, Harold Bloom is quite right when he points to Mary's

enrichment of the Promethean theme by her concentration on the
"equivocal potentialities" inherent in the Titan's symbolic nature.[65]
But we might add that in Byron's short poem these "equivocal
potentialities" are largely ignored while Mary has chosen to employ
in her treatment of the Promethean theme a more genuinely intellectual and philosophical interest than Byron (characteristically)
cared to do. For no matter how well intentioned the bringer of
knowledge may be, he inevitably also brings to mankind the painful
consequence of increased consciousness: an exacerbated capacity to
comprehend man's alienation from the oneness of the truly divine.
And so in her novel Mary links Frankenstein's achievement to
the imagery of Eden and to the sense of loss which followed the
Fall. "You seek for knowledge and wisdom, as I once did," Frankenstein tells Walton; "and I ardently hope that the gratification
of your wishes may not be a serpent to sting you, as mine has
been."[66] And the monster echoes this paradoxical sense of loss-
through-gain, complaining to his creator in a cry that we have come
increasingly to recognize as the anguish of the modern sensibility:
"Increase of knowledge only discovered to me more clearly what
a wretched outcast I was" (Chapter 15).

Furthermore, although a sound argument could easily be made
to view Frankenstein's continuing aspiration (even though defeated
and dying) as a Byronic defiance of "inexorable Heaven," we would
be unfair to the richness of Mary's dual conception not to see also
that Frankenstein's other role—as "Creator"—suggests a most
Shelleyan attitude toward the composite tyranny of the world.

Clearest of all, of course, is the indication that Frankenstein is
far from omnipotent. Like "the erroneous and degrading idea
which men have conceived of a Supreme Being" (preface to *The
Revolt of Islam*) and like the presentation of Jupiter in *Prometheus
Unbound,* the figure of Frankenstein is shown to depart from his
dream of becoming godlike in direct proportion to his failure to
love.[67] Indeed, it is clear that the motive for the creation itself—
the desire in Frankenstein to bring forth "a new species" that
"would bless me as its creator and source" (Chapter 4)—springs
from a spirit within him that wishes to assert its own selfhood over
others. And so, as Frankenstein continues his enumeration of the
advantages of becoming a creator, he declares: "Many happy
and excellent natures would owe their being to me. No father
could claim the gratitude of his child so completely as I should

deserve theirs." In short, what Frankenstein is denying here is the
very principle on which love must rest—that principle which, in
the year of the novel's completion, Shelley was to call "Eldest of
things, divine Equality!"[68]

Consequently, the creation proceeds in a necessarily grotesque
fashion, the Creator viewing his material not with the eyes of love
but with the limited vision of the selfhood, unduly ready to impose
itself by the assertion of "differences" and not "similitudes":[69]

As the minuteness of the parts formed a great hindrance to my speed,
I resolved, contrary to my first intention, to make the being of a gigantic
stature, that is to say, about eight feet in height, and proportionately large.
After having formed this determination and having spent some months
in successfully collecting and arranging my materials, I began. . . .

How can I describe my emotions at this catastrophe, or how delineate the
wretch whom with such infinite pains and care I had endeavoured to form?
His limbs were in proportion, and I had selected his features as beautiful.
Beautiful! Great God! His yellow skin scarcely covered the work of muscles
and arteries beneath; his hair was of a lustrous black, and flowing; his
teeth of a pearly whiteness; but these luxuriances only formed a more horrid contrast with his watery eyes, that seemed almost of the same colour
as the dun-white sockets in which they were set, his shrivelled complexion
and straight black lips. (Chapters 4, 5)

And, when the monster turns upon his creator to reproach him,
the speech he utters reverberates with the full implications of the
ironic version of Genesis that Mary has already given us. "Accursed
creator! Why did you form a monster so hideous that even *you*
turned from me in disgust? God, in pity, made man beautiful and
alluring, after his own image; but my form is a filthy type of yours,
more horrid even from the very resemblance" (Chapter 15). In
other words, a close reading of *Frankenstein* suggests that, even in
the orthodox version of the creation, the deity must be held accountable for a failure of love; for he deliberately (and selfishly)
chose to make man an imperfect image of himself.

And the full Shelleyan strategy of rebuttal—barely implicit
in *Frankenstein* through Victor Frankenstein's dying speech of
continued hope, followed soon afterward by the monster's outburst
of pity for his creator—originates from a conception that is surely
present both in Mary's novel and in Shelley's own poetry: that the
supposed omnipotence of the deity is purely illusory and that his

powers (as well as the powers of all those who simulate his show of dominance) are limited most surely by an imaginative failure to perceive that love, as the eternal principle of life, must lie at the foundation of all things.

A critical reading of *Frankenstein,* then, provides a rich insight into some of the central conflicts of the age that we agree to call Romantic (and, indeed, into some of the most pressing contradictions in Mary Shelley's own mind). On the one hand, the over-all curve of Walton's experience seemingly suggests the futility of aspiration: that man, to use Frankenstein's own words, is wisest when he "believes his native town to be the world." On the other hand, when we look more closely into the novel, we see that the presentation of Victor Frankenstein's character reveals a secondary, subversive theme that itself unfolds into a duality. To speak somewhat unfairly of Mary's achievement, we might say that Frankenstein is presented in his defeat as a Byronic oyster who possibly (and unwittingly) contains a Shelleyan pearl. For, while it is clear that at the end of the novel Frankenstein is portrayed as a radically divided Prometheus who is unable, even on his deathbed, to reconcile man's hopeless conflict between his emotional nature and his intellectual aspirations, it is equally implicit that his true failure stems from the poverty of his imagination and from the inadequacy of his love.

Nor, of course, do such analogues in any sense detract from the stature of *Frankenstein* in its own right. Rather, they indicate the novel's remarkable centrality to an age in which its most brilliant minds were compelled to struggle with a profound sense of conflict: that between an entrenched and powerful system tending toward conservatism in almost every field of human experience (the most concrete example of which was the Congress of Vienna), and an enormous surge of unorganized psychic energy demanding new forms (social, moral, and political) that would be more nearly commensurate with the individual's increased awareness of his needs. And perhaps Shelley himself provides in the preface to *Prometheus Unbound,* the definitive statement on the question of the individual writer's relationship to the climate of his time: "It is impossible that any one who inhabits the same age with such writers as those who stand in the foremost ranks of our own, can conscientiously assure himself that his language and tone of thought may not have been modified by the study of the productions of those extraordinary intellects."—"Extraordinary intellects," indeed, were those two poets who met on the shore of Lake Geneva and who provided, by their very friendship of opposites, the ideational and emotional stimulus to Mary's most famous novel.

VIII *The Godwinian Influence*

Last of all, we have the problem of assessing the influence of Mary's father upon her novel.[70] To the contemporary reviewers, the book was clearly a product of the Godwinian "school,"[71] a connection made manifest by the dedication: "To William Godwin, Author of *Political Justice, Caleb Williams,* etc., These Volumes Are Respectfully Inscribed." But to us, of course, the problem of assessment stems largely from the fact that Shelley himself is just as likely to be the source of a particular analogue as Godwin. One example, I think, should suffice to illustrate the difficulty.

It is obvious that *Paradise Lost* was much in Mary's mind as she worked on *Frankenstein.* Not only does it provide her with her epigraph, but it is also the book which most impresses the monster in the account he gives of his reading in Chapter 15. Indeed, it is evident enough that the questioning of divine "justice" implicit in the novel parallels the reassessment, so characteristic of the age, of Milton's epic. Thus Shelley's view of *Paradise Lost* in the preface to *Prometheus Unbound* indicates approval of Satan's "firm and patient opposition to omnipotent force" and continues with the declaration that Satan is the true "hero" of the poem.[72] Furthermore, we know that Shelley was reading Milton on August 21, 1816—the day he and Mary had their conference about *Frankenstein*—[73] and that in November he read *Paradise Lost* aloud to her.[74] Yet, if we turn to Godwin's *Political Justice,* a work with which Mary was necessarily quite familiar,[75] we find her father evaluating *Paradise Lost* in this fashion:

It has no doubt resulted from a train of speculation similar to this [that is, that "great intellectual power" and "a strong sense of justice" are usually found together], that poetical readers have commonly remarked Milton's devil to be a being of considerable virtue. It must be admitted that his energies centered too much in personal regards. But why did he rebel against his maker? It was, as he himself informs us, because he saw no sufficient reason, for that extreme inequality of rank and power, which

the creator assumed. It was because prescription and precedent form no
adequate ground for implicit faith. After his fall, why did he still cherish the
spirit of opposition? From a persuasion that he was hardly and injuriously
treated. . . . He sought revenge, because he could not think with tameness
of the unexpostulating authority that assumed to dispose of him. How
beneficial and illustrious might the temper from which these qualities
flowed, have been found, with a small diversity of situation![76]

Obviously, to untangle here the strands of possible Godwinian and
Shelleyan influence on Mary would be an impossibility.

And yet, despite this cautionary prelude, it seems possible to
single out a number of probable influences exerted on *Frankenstein*
by Godwin's novels. First, and perhaps most obvious, is the theme
of pursuit in *Caleb Williams* (1794), a theme also markedly present
in the final chapter of *Frankenstein*.[77] Second, from *Caleb Williams*
again, Mary may have derived her concept of the pathos of a crim-
inality which is really the consequence not of individual viciousness
but of social corruption. Thus Falkland, the ostensible villain of
Caleb Williams (and, indeed, a murderer and an oppressor of others),
is presented to us as a figure worthy of genuine compassion; for he
is trapped between his better impulses and society's spurious ideal
of honor—a concept not very different from Mary's portrayal of
the monster as a creature of the most benevolent intentions, driven
into murder by a world unduly concerned with appearances.
Indeed, for Shelley, this concept seemingly was the central moral
point of *Frankenstein*:

Nor are the crimes and malevolence of the single Being [that is, the mon-
ster], though indeed withering and tremendous, the offspring of any un-
accountable propensity to evil, but flow irresistibly from certain causes
fully adequate to their production. They are the children, as it were, of
Necessity and Human Nature. In this the direct moral of the book consists,
and it is perhaps the most important and of the most universal application
of any moral that can be enforced by example—Treat a person ill and he
will become wicked. Requite affection with scorn; let one being be selected
for whatever cause as the refuse of his kind—divide him, a social being,
from society, and you impose upon him the irresistible obligations—malevolence and selfishness.[78]

Third, in Godwin's *St. Leon* (1799), the protagonist is depicted
as having gained access to the secret of immorality, to "the *elixir*

vitae," a striking analogue to Frankenstein's pursuit after, and
discovery of, the secret of life. Moreover, in this novel of Godwin's
certain reflections occur which are noticeably similar in spirit to
the implications of *Frankenstein.* (Scott, it is of some interest to note,
alluded to the resemblance between *Frankenstein* and *St. Leon*
in his review of Mary's novel.)[79] For one thing, in a confrontation
between a mysterious stranger and St. Leon, the stranger tempts
St. Leon to break all human ties for the sake of a splendid achievement: "Feeble and effeminate mortal! . . . Was ever gallant action
atchieved [sic], by him who was incapable of separating himself from
a woman? Was ever a great discovery prosecuted, or an important
benefit conferred upon the human race by him who was incapable
of standing, and thinking, and feeling, alone?"[80] For another,
once St. Leon yields to the temptation, he finds, like Frankenstein,
that the human cost far outweighs the sense of eminence: "Me-
thought the race of mankind looked too insignificant in my eyes.
I felt a degree of uneasiness at the immeasurable distance that was
now put between me and the rest of my species. I found myself
alone in the world."[81] And last, after he has produced the *elixir
vitae* and become immortal, St. Leon breaks out in a cry that might
well have come from the lips of the monster: "I can no longer
cheat my fancy; I know that I am alone. The creature does not
exist with whom I have any common language, or any genuine
sympathies. . . . The nearer I attempt to draw any of the nominal
ties of our nature, the more they start and shrink from my grasp."[82]

But although other analogues could easily be found both in
Godwin's fiction and in his more abstract speculations, the problem
of Shelley's intervening influence dooms such an effort to doubtful
value. And perhaps it may be best to end with a statement from
Maria Vohl, one of Mary's earliest book-length critics—one which
stresses not the similarities between father and daughter, but rather
their essential differences: "Nevertheless [despite similarities] I do
not hesitate to rank *Frankenstein* as artistically superior to all of
Godwin's novels. *Frankenstein* is more than an imitation of Godwin.
The entire tone is different. In *Caleb Williams* and in *St. Leon*
we are always conscious of the cold, clear-headed, matter-of-fact
author, constantly passing judgment and drawing conclusions,
all the while displaying the linking of the occurrences to relentless
Necessity. *Frankenstein,* on the other hand, is permeated with
strong emotion."[83]

CHAPTER 3

Valperga

VALPERGA; or, the Life and Adventures of Castruccio, Prince
of Lucca (1823), Mary's second novel, has hardly fared well
with modern critics. Although one of the most eminent of present-
day Shelleyans, Frederick L. Jones, has praised the book quite
highly, calling it "her best novel" and ranking it well above *Frankenstein*,[1] it is undeniable that such a judgment receives little, if
any, support from other commentators. Sylva Norman, who speaks
of the "persistence" necessary for a reader to get through *Valperga*,
declares, for example, that the novel "harbours some of Mary's
dreariest writing";[2] R. Glynn Grylls, in what is still the best available biography of Mary, dismisses the novel in a line, claiming
that its "literary value . . . is negligible";[3] and Muriel Spark,
although somewhat more generous, still feels that *Valperga* reflects
a serious failure "to assimilate the story within its pattern of superstition, inquisition and ancestral warfare."[4] Even more suggestive,
perhaps, is the fact that of Mary's first three novels, *Valperga*
is the only one unavailable in a modern reprint. Indeed, it is the
only one of Mary's six novels which has never been reprinted in
any form,[5] so that copies of the three-volume set are relatively
difficult to find.

Yet despite the near-unanimity of this negative verdict in contemporary appraisals, the modern reader will probably find his reaction
to *Valperga* much closer to that of Jones than to that of the other
critics. For, although it is easy enough to point to a number of
distracting weaknesses in the book—the self-indulgence of its
excessive length, the vagueness of Castruccio himself, the too-
frequent insertion of historically authentic, fictionally irrelevant
episodes—*Valperga* does seem the most readable of the novels
after *Frankenstein*. Not that it is the "best" of her novels—or, for
that matter, even her second best—but in its characterization,
especially of the figures of Beatrice of Ferrara and Benedetto Pepi,
Mary does reach her highest achievement in that area. Certainly,
at any rate, Shelley himself recognized the book as a significant

advance over *Frankenstein;*[6] and Godwin, hardly the man to indulge in well-meaning flattery, told Mary that *Valperga* struck him as "a work of more genius" than her first novel.[7]

But, in another sense, the critical divergence about *Valperga* seems characteristic of the problems raised by it. Two of those problems, in fact, both of which are significant, appear insoluble. The first concerns the question of Godwin's alterations of Mary's original manuscript; the second arises from a comment of Mary's, made apparently in 1839, which indicates that we lack some essential information about the novel's publication in 1823. But, at this point, a brief account of the background of the book may help to place the two problems in perspective.

I *Composition and Publication*

Valperga is one of those works which seem dogged from the outset by bad luck and personal misfortune for its author. First conceived in the library of the Shelley residence at Marlow in 1817, the book was truly, to use Mary's own description of it, "a child of mighty slow growth,"[8] since it was not completed until the autumn of 1821.[9] In the interim, she suffered the loss of a daughter and of a son in 1818–19;[10] she may well have passed through a severe marital crisis with Shelley in 1818 that altered their relationship drastically;[11] and, if we may judge from the evidence of *Mathilda* (1819), a *novella* left in manuscript until this century, she may have had to struggle with—and eventually exorcise—a strong sense of revulsion toward her father's extremely selfish behavior both in money matters and in his indifference to her own emotional needs. Indeed, at least one critic, Muriel Spark, has found in the novel's background of personal grief a possible explanation for the lack of integration in *Valperga:* during the period of its composition, she feels, Mary was probably too often distraught to create a satisfactory whole.[12]

But, whatever adverse effect the necessarily disjointed method of composition may have had, the extended pattern of Mary's interest in *Valperga* more surely reveals two aspects of her character that are well worth stressing: the seriousness of her aspirations for literary eminence during the earlier stages of her career;[13] and the genuine intellectual thoroughness she brought to her work, a habit she no doubt first absorbed from Godwin[14] but which Shelley must have intensified by his own example. "Mary is writing a

novel, illustrative of the manners of the Middle Ages in Italy,"
Shelley wrote to Peacock in late 1820, "which she has raked out
of fifty old books."[15] And Mary herself, in a letter of 1821, indicates
that her desire to make her study of Castruccio as accurate as possible caused her to delay for some time in beginning the novel:
in the winter of 1818–19, she found some of the necessary materials
at Naples; but she discovered she still needed "other books."
And it was not until 1820, at Pisa, that the actual writing got under
way.[16]

Of course, Shelley's reference to "fifty old books" makes an in-
timidating beginning to anyone interested in Mary's use of source
material for her fourteenth-century setting. Fortunately enough,
the preface to *Valperga* provides us with what we would today call
a "selective bibliography." There Mary contrasts Machiavelli's
"romance" concerning Castruccio with "his real adventures" to
be found in Sismondi's "delightful publication, *Histoire des Républiques Italiennes de l'Age Moyen*," and she then cites two other
studies which she found less useful than Sismondi's: "Tegrino's
Life of Castruccio and Giovanni Villani's *Florentine Annals*."[17]
Furthermore, an examination of these four works reveals that
Mary used them primarily for her background to the period (especially in the political and religious spheres) and for many of the
external details of Castruccio's career; but, for her two major
female characters (Euthanasia and Beatrice), as well as for the
"most romantic"[18] nature of her plot, she was content to rely, to
quote once more from the reviewer in *Blackwood's,* on "thoughts
and feelings, not only modern, but modern and feminine at once."[19]

In fact, with the aid of her journals and letters, we are able to
determine fairly closely the various periods at which Mary was
studying the four works cited in the novel's preface. In January and
February, 1819, when she was at Naples, she read Sismondi, her
major source, and responded to his history with a good deal of
enthusiasm.[20] In the early spring of 1820, she read both Machiavelli's and Niccolò Tegrimi's biographies of Castruccio.[21]
In the autumn of that same year she read Sismondi again, along
with Villani's history of Florence, continuing with the latter through
the winter and into the spring of 1821.[22] And, in July of that year,
with the rough draft nearly complete, she turned to Tegrimi once
more, evidently for a final check upon the details contained in the
earliest biography of Castruccio.[23]

When the novel reached completion in late 1821, however, Mary

again experienced difficulties in attaining publication. This time
the problem was due not so much to any publisher's reluctance
to accept the book but to Mary's own sense of increased worth in
the literary marketplace. Lackington, the publisher of *Frankenstein,*
declined to meet the terms she demanded;[24] and Ollier, Shelley's
own publisher, although evidently interested in the book, proved
exasperatingly indecisive and hesitant in the negotiations.[25]
Finally, in January, 1822, Mary sent the manuscript to her father,
"telling him to make the best of it" and to apply whatever money he
gained from its sale to his own financial needs.[26]

And with these instructions, a major problem arises, for Godwin
felt free to take Mary at even more than her word. "Your novel is
now fully printed, and ready for publication," he wrote to her in
February, 1823. "I have taken great liberties with it, and I am
afraid your *amour propre* will be proportionately shocked."[27]
Naturally, from such a remark as this, the inevitable question follows: how much of Mary's second novel is actually her father's
work? To Muriel Spark, the answer can only be one of uncertainty:
"*Valperga* was intruded upon by Godwin's editing of it, to what
extent of patchwork we cannot know";[28] while Sylva Norman
drily dismisses the question (along with the novel) by remarking
that we ought to "thank Godwin for the liberties he took with it."[29]

But, although we are condemned to remain in the area of con-
jecture regarding the extent of Godwin's alterations, there are clues
enough to warrant a reasonable guess as to the relative significance
of what was done to the manuscript after it had left Mary's hands.
For one thing, Godwin hastened to assure his daughter that "all
the merit of the book is exclusively your own. The *whole* of what
I have done is merely confined to taking away things which must
have prevented its success."[30] And, for another, this implication
that the changes were largely restricted to matters of excision appears confirmed by a second letter of Godwin's, written to Mary
shortly before the novel's publication:

Perhaps it may be of some use to you if I give you my opinion of *Castruccio.*
I think there are parts of high genius, and that your two females are ex-
ceedingly interesting; but I am not satisfied. *Frankenstein* was a fine thing;
it was compressed, muscular, and firm; nothing relaxed and weak; no
proud flesh. *Castruccio* is a work of more genius; but it appears, in reading,
that the first rule you prescribed to yourself was, I will let it be long. It contains the quantity of four volumes of *Waverley.* No hard blow was ever hit
with a woolsack![31]

In short, it seems likely that Godwin's intrusion upon the manuscript was no more (and probably something less) than the assistance many modern novelists receive from their editors.

When *Valperga* was published in February, 1823, the reviews were generally favorable.[32] *Blackwood's* was again generous in the amount of space it allotted to Mary, its notice of the novel running to eleven pages and including several lengthy extracts. "Our chief objection," the reviewer declared,

> may be summed up in one word—Mrs. Shelley has not done justice to the character of Castruccio. . . . [However,] laying out of view [Castruccio's] real life and character, we can have no hesitation in saying, that Mrs. Shelley has given us a clever and amusing romance. . . . By far the most striking part of this history . . . and indeed we may add, by far the finest part of the book, is that in which the loves of Castruccio and Euthanasia are broken and disturbed by those of Castruccio and a certain Beatrice of Ferrara. . . . The work . . . undoubtedly reflects no *discredit* even on the authoress of *Frankenstein.*[33]

Even the *Literary Chronicle,* ordinarily quite hostile to productions tainted in any way by contact with Shelley and his circle, praised *Valperga* highly and predicted that the novel would outlive its own day.[34] Perhaps such praise from such quarters led Mary to make her puzzled comment to Maria Gisborne after the reviews had begun appearing: "I am surprised that none of the Literary Gazettes are shocked."[35]

But, in spite of so promising a reception, *Valperga* apparently met with a mysterious mishap shortly after publication. In May, 1823, Godwin wrote to Mary that five hundred copies of the original impression of one thousand had been sold since February,[36] a hardly discouraging rate of sale. More than a decade later, however, after Mary's career as a novelist had ended (her sixth, and last, novel, *Falkner,* had appeared in 1837), we find her lamenting *Valperga* "never had fair play; never being properly published."[37] For such a remark as this, of course, two interpretations seem possible. The first—and the one which seems to have been universally accepted—is that Mary is merely expressing the traditional complaint of the hard-working author who feels his labor has gone without proper recognition. But, although this may well be the case, there does seem to be enough circumstantial evidence to bolster the likelihood of a second possibility: that misfortune

dogged *Valperga* to the very end, even after its publisher—G. and
W. B. Whittaker—had issued the book.

There are several reasons for suspecting this state of affairs.
The most persuasive reason of all, perhaps, arises from the curious
fact that *Valperga* alone of Mary's six novels has never been reprinted—despite, as we have seen, the favorable reception accorded to it at its appearance. And, if we examine more closely
the events of 1823, the year of the novel's publication, we are able
to find two specific areas in which an answer may reside to the
problem raised by Mary's later complaint. In the summer of that
year Godwin asked Whittaker to publish quickly a second edition
of *Frankenstein* in the hopes of capitalizing on the temporary
success of a play *(Presumption)* which had been based on Mary's
first novel.[38] Whether this diversion of the publisher's energy
away from *Valperga* had something to do with Mary's subsequent
feeling of hard usage we cannot know for certain—but that it
may have is surely a possibility.

Furthermore, the nature of Mary's own actions after she returned
to England in August seems to present another, perhaps more
plausible, solution to her remark that *Valperga* "never had fair
play." Almost at once she wrote to her father-in-law, Sir Timothy
Shelley, in the hopes of gaining an allowance from him for herself
and her son.[39] Negotiations, begun in earnest in early September
with Godwin present,[40] continued throughout the autumn of
1823; and, although many of the crucial letters are evidently lost,[41]
there is a definite possibility that Sir Timothy, already embittered
by the obituary notices accorded his son,[42] had something to say
about *Valperga* and the reviews it was receiving—reviews in which
Shelley's name appeared and in which his ideas suffered their usual
share of resentment and travesty.[43] Certainly, at any rate, Sir
Timothy showed no hesitation in 1824 (with the publication of
the *Posthumous Poems)* and in 1826 (when the reviews of *The Last
Man* mentioned Mary by name) in insisting that Shelley's name
be kept out of the public notice, going so far in 1824 as to buy 191
copies of his son's *Posthumous Poems.*[44] Nor should we forget
that the financially desperate Godwin—who held the copyright
to *Valperga*—was an interested party throughout the negotiations
with Sir Timothy. In short, the question must remain an open one;
but I cannot help wondering whether it has received the attention it
deserves. From its adequate solution, in fact, coupled to our aware-

ness of Mary's undoubted difficulties with Sir Timothy over the publication of *The Last Man,* may spring a valuable insight into the problem of Mary Shelley's marked decline as a novelist.

II *The Novel*

Any attempt to describe the contents of *Valperga* should begin with Shelley's letter to Charles Ollier (his own publisher), in which, in the course of negotiations which were eventually to prove abortive, Shelley provided an indispensable outline:

The romance is called *Castruccio, Prince of Lucca,* and is founded (not upon the novel of Machiavelli under that name, which substitutes a childish fiction for the far more romantic truth of history, but) upon the actual story of his life. He was a person who, from an exile and an adventurer, after having served in the wars of England and Flanders in the reign of our Edward the Second, returned to his native city, and, liberating it from its tyrants, became himself its tyrant, and died in the full splendour of his dominion, which he had extended over the half of Tuscany. He was a little Napoleon, and, with a dukedom instead of an empire for his theatre, brought upon the same all the passions and errors of his antitype. The chief interest of the romance rests upon Euthanasia, his betrothed bride, whose love for him is only equalled by her enthusiasm for the liberty of the republic of Florence, which is in some sort her country, and for that of Italy, to which Castruccio is a devoted enemy, being an ally of the party of the Emperor [Henry VII, d. 1313; then Louis IV]. This character is a masterpiece; and the key-stone of the drama, which is built up with admirable art, is the conflict between these passions and these principles. Euthanasia, the last survivor of a noble house, is a feudal countess, and her castle is the scene of the exhibition of the knightly manners of the time. The character of Beatrice, the prophetess, can only be done justice to in the very language of the author. I know nothing in Walter Scott's novels which at all approaches to the beauty and sublimity of this—creation, I may almost say, for it is perfectly original; and, although founded upon the ideas and manners of the age which is represented, is wholly without a similitude in any fiction I ever read. Beatrice is in love with Castruccio and dies; for the romance, although interspersed with much lighter matter, is deeply tragic, and the shades darken and gather as the catastrophe approaches. All the manners, customs, opinions, of the age are introduced; the superstitions, the heresies, and the religious persecutions are displayed; the minutest circumstances of Italian manners in that age is not omitted; and the whole seems to me to constitute a living and a moving picture of an age almost forgotten.[45]

Although we may be tempted to make some deduction from Shelley's enthusiasm on the grounds of the obvious purpose of his letter—to interest Ollier in purchasing *Valperga*—his summary account is a valuable indication of the best method of approaching Mary's long, second novel.

Quite clearly, as Shelley indicates, there are three major characters—Castruccio himself, who, in the course of the plot, develops into a bloody tyrant; Euthanasia, his childhood companion, who is still deeply in love with Castruccio during the earlier stages of his career; and Beatrice of Ferrara, an extremely beautiful, religiously deluded girl with whom Castruccio has a brief affair. Within such a pattern of emphasis, we most surely find the true nature of Mary's interest: the feminization of her material in order to impose value judgments on what was in actuality a most unfeminine age—as well as, if we may judge from the sources cited in the preface, the most unsentimental career of Castruccio. But, at this point, a closer description of the plot of *Valperga* is useful.

Somewhere around the year 1290 (according to Mary's chronology),[46] Castruccio is born to a prominent Ghibelline family of Lucca. By the time he is eleven, he and his parents are exiled by the victorious Guelph party. By the time he is seventeen, he is an orphan—and, shortly after this stage has been reached in his career, Castruccio may be said to take his first uncertain step toward prominence. Living with the benevolent Francis Guinigi, Castruccio is advised, if he truly does desire fame, to seek it outside Italy. Castruccio, who acts on this advice, lands in England in 1309 during the reign of Edward II.

Despite royal favor, Castruccio destroys all prospect of advancement in England by killing a noble during a petty quarrel. He flees to Ostend and shortly afterward meets the first dark angel of his career, Alberto Scoto, who is in command of a mercenary army in Flanders. Scoto, himself a crafty unscrupulous man, introduces Castruccio (who, of course, is still quite impressionable) to the trickery and deceit necessary in the world of successful power politics: "Hitherto [Castruccio's] mind had been innocence, and all his thoughts were honour. Frankness played on his lips; ingenuousness nestled in his heart; shame was ever ready to check him on the brink of folly; and the tenderness of his nature seemed to render it impossible for him to perpetrate a deed of harshness or inhumanity. . . . But nineteen is a dangerous age; and ill betides the youth who confides himself to a crafty instructor" (I, 94–95).

Influenced by Scoto's advice, Castruccio returns to Italy to participate in the Ghibelline resurgence of power. There, in 1313–14, he allies himself with Ugoccione della Faggiuola for the purpose of restoring Ghibelline control over Lucca, his native city. At this point, however, Euthanasia (who, two years Castruccio's junior, is now twenty-two) begins to play a prominent role in the novel. An orphan herself, she lives at Valperga, a castle in the Apennines; and she experiences "deep pain" when she learns that Castruccio, her childhood friend, has become the "betrayer of his country" (I, 166). Or, restated in terms of the factional disputes of medieval Italy, Castruccio, by actively aligning himself with the imperial interests of the age (the Ghibellines, who favor the cause of the Holy Roman Emperor), poses a dangerous threat to the republican party (that is, the Guelphs), of whom Euthanasia is an ardent champion. And it is here, of course, as Shelley's letter to Ollier indicates, that we have the major conflict of the book: the struggle between Euthanasia's love for Castruccio and her desire that the cause of liberty should prevail in Italy.

The remainder of the novel deals with the increasing degradation of Castruccio's moral character until he has "in truth become a tyrant" (III, 14) with "cruelty . . . an elemental feature" of his makeup (III, 170). In this respect, then, the summary statement given to his development by the reviewer in *Blackwood's* is undoubtedly an accurate one: "The attempt, whether successful or not, is certainly made to depict the slow and gradual formation of a crafty and bloody Italian tyrant of the middle ages, out of an innocent, open-hearted, and deeply feeling youth."[47]

But such an assessment is incomplete unless we also recognize Mary's strategy of representing Castruccio's decline: by showing, through the downward curve of Euthanasia's love for him, the loss of whatever noble qualities Castruccio once possessed. Thus, at the dawning of her attachment, "she made a god of him she loved, believing every virtue and every talent to live in his soul" (I, 189). In the final volume, however, when Euthanasia examines her emotional attitude toward the tyrannical figure that Castruccio has become, she discovers that it is "neither hatred, nor revenge, nor contempt; . . . she felt grief alone" (III, 65–67). Indeed, the most remarkable character in the book, Beatrice of Ferrara, provides much the same effect as Euthanasia in helping the reader experience a concrete sense of Castruccio's decline. For, like Euthanasia, Beatrice begins by loving Castruccio, making of him, because of her own religious delusion, something analogous to a messenger sent from God (II, 87–88). And, although Beatrice continues to love Castruccio until her death, it is evident that his seduction of her (soon followed by his conscious decision to abandon her in order to further his political ambitions), her subsequently degraded vision of life (at one point she asserts her belief in "the eternal and victorious influence of evil" [III, 44]), and her deluded end (she dies in a delirium after having taken henbane)—all of these details clearly drive home, as no abstract statement could, the corruptive force of Castruccio's character in the world of *Valperga*. As a result, it is perfectly appropriate that the novel truly ends, not with the death of Castruccio, but with the loss of Euthanasia at sea during a storm:[48] when the moral standard of *Valperga* vanishes in the person of Euthanasia, Castruccio's career becomes meaningless.

III *The Theme of Political Ambition*

From even so brief a summary as this one, it is evident, I think, that Mary Shelley, in her second novel as well as in her first, is interested in taking up the theme of ambition and exploring the emotional cost it exacts. But if *Frankenstein* may be regarded as a religious and even a philosophical treatment of such a theme, then surely *Valperga,* based on an historical figure of medieval Italy, is a political exploration of the same basic dilemma: the conflict between intense aspiration (the desire for political power) and the demands of the human heart. In truth, although Mary's criticism of religious orthodoxy is unmistakable in *Valperga* through the character of Beatrice,[49] one of the weaknesses in the construction of the novel as a whole is that the religious elements never really—as they do in *Frankenstein*—become a part of the central theme. Instead, what we find in *Valperga* is that political issues clearly dominate the formal structure, while the religious criticism—despite its vividness—stands to one side as a brilliant but often irrelevant digression.

Nor is it surprising that political issues should play so large a part in Mary's second novel. For one thing, as we know, *Valperga* was first conceived in 1817, when Shelley was engaged in composing his longest poem, *The Revolt of Islam,* a passionate attempt to indicate the reasons for the failure of the greatest political movement of the age—the French Revolution. Indeed, there is an interesting (if somewhat distorted) echo from Shelley's poem in *Valperga,* one which may possibly explain Mary's choice of Castruccio for the subject of her novel. In *The Revolt of Islam,* the first canto presents an allegoric vision of a fierce struggle between a serpent and an eagle. Contrary to our usual associations, however, we soon learn that the serpent is the "great Spirit of Good" and that the eagle is "the Spirit of Evil"; the latter, in truth, is none other than the "Fiend of blood" which lies at the root of the world's misery.[50] In Mary's novel, as she tells us in the second volume, the crest of Castruccio's house (the Antelminelli) is the eagle; and he hopes to unite it with the crest of the viper (the house of the Visconti) in order to crush Florence, the city which is one of the major symbols for the cause of liberty in *Valperga.*[51] "But no more of this," Castruccio writes to his potential ally in the subjection of Florence; "you know my plans [to rule Florence]; and, if the viper and the eagle unite in firm accord, surely both her heel and her head may receive a deadly wound" (II, 134–35).

For another, both Shelley's subsequent poetry and Mary's own correspondence reveal how deeply the two of them were concerned with political matters during the period Mary was researching and writing *Valperga.* In late 1818, for example, Shelley's "Lines Written among the Euganean Hills" predicts the downfall of Austrian imperialism in Italy (cf. Castruccio and the Ghibelline interests). In 1819, aside from the completion of his masterpiece, *Prometheus Unbound,* Shelley also wrote a series of overtly topical poems on the political situation of England—"Lines Written during the Castlereagh Administration," "The Mask of Anarchy," "Song to the Men of England," and so forth—as well as the long prose essay on political theory, "A Philosophical View of Reform," and a short ode to the Spanish people exhorting them to rise up against their oppressors.[52]

But, perhaps even more importantly, in 1820, when Mary began the actual composition of *Valperga,* political events on the Continent filled her and Shelley's heads with hopes that the reactionary forces of the post-Napoleonic period were declining. "I suppose . . . that you have heard the news," Mary wrote to Maria Gisborne soon after Spain had passed through a bloodless revolution at the start of that year; "the Beloved Ferdinand has proclaimed the Constitution of 1812 & called the Cortes—The Inquisition is abolished [in *Valperga,* it is of some interest to note,

the Italian Inquisition plays an important role in Beatrice's fate]—
The dungeons opened & the Patriots pouring out—This is good.
I should like to be in Madrid now."[53] And in August, not long
after Naples had achieved its own bloodless revolution, Mary
wrote to her friend Amelia Curran: "How enraged all our mighty
rulers are at the quiet revolutions which have taken place."[54]

But even before events in Spain and Italy caused Mary to take
overt notice of the republican movements in these countries, she
had been following political developments in England (or
"Castlereagh land," as she called it) so closely that she half apologized to a friend, in a letter to London of February, 1820, for
running on so about the evils of Castlereagh's administration:
"You see what a John or rather Joan Bull I am so full of politics."[55]
(A perhaps unconscious echo of this remark occurs in the novel itself
when Castruccio observes to one of his evil advisers: "Ah! Messer
Benedetto, you are ever the same . . . ever immersed in politics"
[I, 278–79].)

And, in truth, almost everything in Mary's life seemingly con-
spired to lead her into writing a second novel with a political theme.
Even so early as June, 1818, for example, when the original plan
for *Valperga* lay fallow with much of the research yet to be done,
Godwin wrote to Shelley from England to urge acceptance by
Mary of a discarded idea of his own: to compose a series of biographies that would be called "The Lives of the Commonwealth's
Men," a collection that would deal inevitably with the political
conflicts of seventeenth-century England. "Now this work I shall
never write," Godwin confessed to Shelley. "Mary, perhaps would
like to write it." And the major value of such a book, Godwin
continued, would be that it would help to combat the "strong and
inveterate prejudice in this country in favour of what these heroes
[that is, men like Sir Henry Vane, Milton, Algernon Sidney] styled
'the government of a single person.'"[56]

Whether or not Godwin's letter played a part in confirming
Mary in her plan to write a novel about Castruccio, it is undeniable
that *Valperga* deals with a central figure who schemes to bring
about "the government of a single person." Quite early in the novel,
in fact, when Castruccio is still essentially a boy, Mary makes this
intent clear. He has taken up residence with Francis Guinigi, a
man who, although once a successful military leader, has laid
"aside the distinctions of society" and has turned to agriculture as

a way of life, recognizing, "with lovely humility, . . . the affinity
of the meanest peasant to his own noble mind" (I, 44). Castruccio,
however, argues with Guinigi, endeavoring to prove to him "that
in the present distracted state of mankind, it was better that one
man should get the upper hand, to rule the rest" (I, 49). In other
words, what Mary presents through Castruccio is the fatal result
of the obvious solution to "the present distracted state" of nineteenth-century Europe: the government of each nation by a powerful individual, who is ultimately responsible to no one but himself.

Or, to refine Castruccio's statement still further, the argument he
offers in *Valperga* is very little different from the "solution" offered
by Metternich at the Congress of Vienna in 1814–15: that any kind
of order, even the most tyrannically imposed, is infinitely preferable
to the absence of traditional hierarchies. And the topical nature of
Mary's intention is made clear by Guinigi's answer, for it is also
Shelley's rebuttal to the reactionary tactics of the Quadruple
Alliance: " 'Yes,' said Guinigi, 'let one man, if it be forbidden
to more than one, get the upper hand in wisdom, and let him teach
the rest: teach them the valuable arts of peace and love' " (I, 49).

But this early disputation between Castruccio and Guinigi is
also valuable for pointing to Mary's method of organizing her
political theme. For what she does is present, as stages in Castruccio's
development, a series of dialectic milestones in which Castruccio's
colloquist functions somewhat in the fashion of either the good
or the bad angel in the old morality plays. Guinigi, for example,
is obviously a "good" angel—the first, in fact, that Castruccio
encounters—just as Euthanasia is the most important. Alberto
Scoto, on the other hand, is the first of Castruccio's "bad" angels,
for he introduces Castruccio to the unscrupulous methods of successful power politics. Thus Scoto advises Castruccio, in a Machia-
vellian passage, "But, having once formed an army, disciplined
it, and shewn its temper by success, then is the time to change the
arts of war for those of counsel, and to work your way as the mole,
shewing no sign of your path, until your triumphant power comes
forth where it is least expected" (I, 96). "And in those days," Mary
continues by way of summary of Scoto's effect, "the seeds of craft
were sown, that, flourishing afterwards, contributed to his advancement to power and glory" (I, 101).

Although Scoto, as the first, is the crucial dark angel in Castruccio's career, Benedetto Pepi, whom Castruccio meets in the Alps

while traveling to Italy, is the one receiving the fullest treatment. "An emperor just!" Pepi cries in astonishment at Castruccio's unsophisticated question concerning the policy of Henry VII toward Italy, "a prince impartial! Do not thrones rest upon dissensions and quarrels? And must there not be weakness in the people to create power in the prince?" (I, 116–17). After this outburst, Pepi berates the party of liberty in Italy, the Guelphs: "These republicans, whom from my soul I detest, have turned out the Ghibellines, and are now fighting with the nobles, and asserting the superiority of the vulgar, till every petty artizan of the meanest lane fancies himself as great a prince as the emperor Henry himself. . . . Their watchword is that echo of fools, and laughing stock of the wise,—Liberty. Surely the father of lies invented that bait, that trap at which the multitude catch as a mouse at a bit of cheese" (I, 119). And, by way of emphasis, Pepi adds a summary piece of advice to Castruccio: "My friend, the world, trust me, will never go well, until the rich rule, and the vulgar sink to their right station as slaves of the soil" (I, 124).

Indeed, Pepi, in a striking (although undoubtedly coincidental) similarity to Blake's "The Human Abstract," presents an image of the perdurable nature of human selfishness that seems to insure the perpetuation of injustice: "Tyranny is a healthy tree, it strikes a deep root, and each year its branches grow larger and larger, and its shade spreads wider and wider. While liberty is a word, a breath, an air; it will dissipate, and Florence become as slavish as it is now rebellious; did not Rome fall" (I, 127). As a result, the final stage of Castruccio's moral collapse is indicated by an appropriate reference to his having become indistinguishable from his archtempter: "He now fully subscribed to all the articles of Pepi's political creed, and thought fraud and secret murder fair play, when it thinned the ranks of the enemy" (II, 197).

But, as I have indicated, not only Guinigi but also Euthanasia stands against the malign influences on Castruccio's career. In one of their earliest colloquies, in fact, Euthanasia attempts to rescue Castruccio from the temptation of a self-centered tyranny by suggesting to him that true fulfillment is impossible without a climate of liberty: "The essence of freedom is that clash and struggle which awaken the energies of our nature, and that operation of the elements of our mind, which as it were gives us the force and power that hinder us from degenerating, as they say all things earthly do when not regenerated by change" (I, 197). Again, not long afterward, she breaks out in an impassioned speech that would seem to be an echo of Shelley's "Ode to Liberty," written in early 1820: "If time had not shaken the light of poetry and of genius from his wings, all the past would be dark and trackless; now we have a track—the glorious foot-marks of liberty" (I, 197).[57]

And yet, as we know, the nature of Mary's historical material dooms Euthanasia to failure. No matter how well she may argue, no matter how passionately she may champion the cause of liberty— and at times Euthanasia does indeed justify Claire Clairmont's description of her (a "Shelley in female attire")[58]—Castruccio nevertheless continues his downward path until he amply merits in the novel the harsh summary he receives from the historian cited by Mary as her major source:

> During the fifteen years that he governed Lucca, he gave many proofs of the cruelty of his character. Those that were suspected by him he delivered over to frightful tortures, and his enemies he punished by brutal executions. Always desirous of new subordinates and of new allies, he failed completely to remember those who had helped him during his past needs; he even seemed to rage against them with greater cruelty, as if to acquit himself of the obligation he had contracted. To the Quartigiani he owed his first rise, and we have seen that he made them perish by an appalling execution. Another family of Lucca, the Poggi, had rescued him from the hands of Neri de Faggiuola, and had opened the road to his sovereignty; he seized the opportunity of a private quarrel in which they were engaged in order to behead two of them.[59]

As a result, with Euthanasia's failure of persuasion a foregone conclusion, the task which confronted Mary was that of showing how Castruccio's ostensible political success is nothing more than a hollow victory since it is purchased at the cost of his essential humanity—and such a theme inevitably carries us back to the obvious moral of Victor Frankenstein's development. For, like Frankenstein (and, in truth, also like Walton), Castruccio indulges himself "in dreams of . . . distinction" at an early age (I, 19). Consequently, by the time he becomes an orphan in his seventeenth year and goes to reside with Guinigi, he is already predisposed against the older man's willingness to recognize "the affinity of the meanest peasant" to himself. And his very refusal to acknowledge the principle of equality starts Castruccio not only on the downward path to tyranny but to a condition of increasing emotional deprivation.

For this reason Mary quite clearly places so great an emphasis on "romantic" (to quote the reviewer in *Blackwood's* again), nonhistorical elements in her narrative. Not once, but twice Castruccio rejects a specific love which is offered to him—first, from Euthanasia; then, from Beatrice. For, while Castruccio persists in his offer to marry Euthanasia, she refuses to accept anyone who is an enemy to liberty, regardless of how deep her love for Castruccio may be (I, 213). Thus Castruccio has his own interior conflict, although the concentration on Euthanasia's emotional reactions tends to muffle it. "Ambition," we are told in the second volume, shortly before Euthanasia informs Castruccio that she must break with him, "and the fixed desire to rule, smothered in his mind the voice of better reason; and the path of tyranny was smoothed, by his steady resolve to obtain the power, which under one form or another it had been the object of his life to obtain" (II, 146).

Furthermore, this implicit struggle in Castruccio between his ambitious dreams of power and his love for Euthanasia is given direct expression in the account of the aftereffects of his brief affair with Beatrice: "And love was with him, ever after, the second feeling in his heart, the servant and thrall of his ambition" (II, 174). And the consequences of this triumph of political ambition over the needs of the human heart receive their baldest expression at the end of the novel when, with Euthanasia dead, Castruccio meets again one of the dark angels of his youth, Galeazzo Visconti:

> In recording the events which had passed since their separation, Galeazzo found, that, if he had lost sovereignty and power, Castruccio had lost that which might be considered far more valuable; he had lost his dearest friends. ... We know nothing of the private communion of these friends; but we may guess that, if Castruccio revealed the sorrows of his heart, Galeazzo might have regretted that, instead of having instigated the ambition, and destroyed the domestic felicity of his friend, he had not taught him other lessons, through which he might have enjoyed that peace, sympathy and happiness, of which he was now for ever deprived. (III, 266–67)

What we have in *Valperga,* then, is the portrayal of a man who chooses power and personal eminence in preference to love. And, like Victor Frankenstein, Castruccio finds that even the limited achievement of his dream of eminence traps him in a selfhood of exacerbated isolation: like Frankenstein's monster, Castruccio's ambition takes on a murderous autonomy of its own:

> It were curious to mark the changes that now operated in [Castruccio's] character. Every success made him extend his views to something beyond; and every obstacle surmounted, made him still more impatient of those that presented themselves in succession. He became all in all to himself; his creed seemed to contain no article but the end and aim of his ambition; and that he swore before heaven to attain. Accustomed to see men die in battle for his cause, he became callous to blood, and felt no more whether it flowed for his security on a scaffold, or in the field of honour; and every new act of cruelty hardened his heart for those to come. (II, 171)

So it is, that at the end of the novel, with Euthanasia reduced to a captured member of the utterly defeated republican party, she can still assert to the victorious Castruccio the moral point of his ostensibly successful career: that his life is "miserable" and "unworthy"—while Castruccio, driven for the moment into the clarity of a genuine insight, can do nothing more than agree (III, 248–50). In short, in the scheme of *Valperga,* Castruccio, like the Jupiter of *Prometheus Unbound,* is shown to be struggling to retain less than what his victims already possess: the cost of a system of political inequality permeates an entire society, ultimately redounding, in its emotional consequences, upon the tyrant himself. And although analogues drawn from actuality may be less illuminating than ingenious, I doubt if anyone, fresh from a reading of the memoirs of Stalin's daughter, Svetlena Alliluyeva, will be inclined to accuse Mary Shelley of naïveté.

IV *The Reassessment of Heroism*

But the theme of political ambition, coupled as it is in *Valperga* with the military elements of Castruccio's career, inevitably led Mary into another major concern of the period. Indeed, it is possible to perceive in the last-minute change in the novel's title—from *Castruccio, Prince of Lucca* to *Valperga*—a highly suggestive point of departure. For Valperga, as we have seen, is not a character in the novel at all but is the name of the castle in the Apennines where the orphaned Euthanasia dwells. As such, then, the change in title (regardless of who was responsible for it)[60] reflects quite

neatly the thrust of Mary's intention: to show the wisdom of do-
mesticating those forces which go into the marking of a Castruccio—
or, to use Shelley's phrase from his letter to Ollier, which go into
the making of "a little Napoleon."

When we recognize this intention, a genuinely significant aspect
of Mary's novel becomes clear: like her greater contemporaries,
she was engaged in *Valperga* in a reassessment of the concept
of heroism. For, as Brian Wilkie has observed in his valuable
study of the epic tradition in the Romantic period, such a reassessment was felt to be a crucial task for the age:

> When we examine the fortunes of heroism in the Romantic age we become
> aware of . . . a problem in definition. For heroism . . . can mean more than
> one thing. One meaning stresses virility; by this criterion the hero need
> not be moral but must be bold, strong, extroverted. . . . The other meaning
> is almost the exact opposite; here heroism is the quality of high and essential
> humanity—in the etymological sense, "kindness." . . . It is primarily
> because they saw the problem . . . that the Romantics used the epic form or
> epic elements so seriously, for the relationship of modern heroism to older
> versions of it could best be shown by pouring the new wine into old bottles. [61]

Thus Shelley, as Wilkie remarks of *The Revolt of Islam* (1818),
"rejects the martial element in heroism, though he adopts the
military metaphor"; [62] while Byron, as a glance at the opening
of *Don Juan* shows, begins his masterpiece by drily dismissing
the period's conventional methods for defining the heroic man:

> *I want a hero: an uncommon want,*
> *When every year and month sends forth a new one,*
> *Till, after cloying the gazettes with cant,*
> *The age discovers he is not the true one.*

And so it is in *Valperga*, where, granted the necessarily lower
intensity of a long prose fiction, we find Mary evaluating Castruccio's
career and then firmly rejecting all suggestion that military valor
or political success is enough to constitute a "hero." Perhaps for
this reason she even dismisses Machiavelli's account of Castruccio
as a "romance." For to Machiavelli, Castruccio

was one of those, who, considering the place where he was born, and the
time in which he lived, performed very great and extraordinary things: for

he was neither more happy nor eminent in his birth, than many other Heroes.
. . . He was . . . full of wiles and strategems when he had enemies to deal
with; . . . as he used to say, that success, by what means soever procured,
was equally glorious. No man ever took wiser measures to prevent difficulties and dangers, or behaved with more intrepidity and presence of mind
when they could not be avoided: for it was a maxim with him, that a man
ought to try all things, and be dismayed at nothing. . . . Having equalled
the great actions of Philip of Macedon, and Scipio the Roman, he died at
the same age that they did; and if he had been born at either Rome or
Macedon, instead of Lucca, it is very probable he would have far surpassed
them both.[63]

To Mary, however, as we can gather from Euthanasia's remarks,
Castruccio, through his rejection of the social and domestic virtues,
is the very reverse of a hero. "What is the world, except what we
feel?" Euthanasia says to Castruccio at one point. "Love, and
hope, and delight, or sorrow and tears; these are our lives, our
realities, to which we give the names of power, possession, misfortune, and death" (I, 193). And this assertion of the supremacy
of the life of the emotions is given an unmistakable domestic turn
in Euthanasia's later wish to restore the lost nobility of Castruccio's
character by teaching him to "love obscurity" (III, 205–6). Indeed,
in a remarkable parallel to *Prometheus Unbound*, Euthanasia's
home becomes a symbol of the last bastion of liberty and hope
in the world of *Valperga:* "Of the castles which were situated within
a circuit of many miles around Lucca, all were subject to Castruccio,
except the castle of Valperga and its dependencies. He had often
solicited Euthanasia to place her lordship under the protection of
his government; and she had uniformly refused" (II, 203). In
Prometheus Unbound, Shelley begins his masterpiece with Prometheus apostrophizing the composite tyranny of the world:

> *Monarch of Gods and Daemons, and all Spirits*
> *But one [Prometheus himself], who throng these*
>   *bright and rolling worlds*
> *Which Thou and I alone of living things*
> *Behold with sleepless eyes! regard this Earth*
> *Made multitudinous with thy slaves.)*

Nor do I think I am at all exaggerating the scope of Mary's
design in *Valperga*. On January 12, 1820, when she was about to

begin the actual writing, she sent to Maria Gisborne a letter which
provides an invaluable clue to the center of her novel:

> Are you yet reconciled to the idea that England is become a despotism?
> The freedom with which the newspapers talk of our most detestable govern-
> ors is as mocking death on a death bed. The work of dissolution goes on,
> not a whit the slower. And cannot England be saved? I do hope it will.
> . . . We have fallen, I fear, on evil days. There are great spirits in England.
> So there were in the time of Caesar at Rome. Athens flourished but just
> before the despotism of Alexander. Will all England fall? I am full of
> these thoughts.[64]

That is, by choosing to write a novel about a figure who, judged by
earlier standards, might be deemed a hero, by further choosing to
show the superiority of liberty and of the domestic virtues and of
the absence of personal ambition, as well as by emphasizing the
essential emptiness of Castruccio's life, Mary played her part—
nor was it an ignoble one—in perhaps the most important effort of
nineteenth-century English literature: to attempt to channel the
eddying currents of a disrupted society into a stable relationship
with permanent human values.

   Although we can only speculate as to the reasons for such a widespread concern in the reassessment of heroism during the period,
it would seem—to narrow our investigation for the moment to
Mary and Shelley—that at least a partial answer lies in the frightening implications of the aftermath of the French Revolution and the
rise of Napoleon. Thus Shelley, who, as we have seen, specifically
likens Castruccio to Napoleon, remarks in his "Philosophical
View of Reform" that all lovers of liberty were first, "struck as
with palsy" by the "usurpation of Bonaparte" and were then grat-
ified by the complete failure of "the military project of government
of the great tyrant."[65] From this remark of Shelley's we can, in
conjunction with the obvious impress Napoleon had upon the age,
deduce a conclusion of somewhat wider application: at a time when
the most acute minds of the period were absorbing, each in his
own way, the realization that the old orthodoxies were no longer
capable of satisfying the expanded demands of individual consciousness, Napoleon had unmistakably demonstrated one terrifying
"solution": nationalism as a kind of religious force, with a figure
of absolutism at its head, guiding it along a path of military ex-

pansion. And, of course, this potential "solution", unhappily and starkly, confronts us even today.

Certainly, to narrow our discussion again, Mary was herself aware of the peculiar dangers implicit in the new kind of political consciousness revealed by the French Revolution. "This alliance with foreign governments," she wrote in an analysis of the earlier stages of the revolution, "and the complicity of the court with the emigrants, roused a spirit in France, at first noble and heroic, till, led away by base and sanguinary men, grandeur of purpose merged into ferocity, and heroism became a thirst of blood such as mankind had never displayed before. . . ."[66] And again, during her biographical sketch of Ugo Foscolo, she observed: "Men need a career—an hope, an aim; the French revolution first gave new life to these natural instincts, and then, aided by Napoleon's despotism, tore them up."[67] In *Valperga,* which was written more than a decade before these remarks, we can still discover, beneath the prolixities and the sentimentalities, a genuinely creative sensibility earnestly at work in the hope of destroying the Napoleonic danger at its source.

CHAPTER 4

The Last Man

FOR some time it has been recognized by commentators that *The Last Man* (1826) represents a creative landmark in Mary Shelley's career—a landmark which has been obscured both by the fame of *Frankenstein* and by her role as Shelley's wife. As early as 1891, for example, Richard Garnett, in his introduction to Mary's *Tales and Stories,* excepted *The Last Man* from his general complaint that the novels after *Frankenstein* all show a distinct falling off:

> *The Last Man* demands great attention, for it is not only a work of far higher merit than commonly admitted, but of all her works the most characteristic of the authoress, the most representative of Mary Shelley in the character of pining widowhood which it was her destiny to support for the remainder of her life. . . . The languor which mars her other writings is a beauty here, harmonizing with the general tone of sublime melancholy. . . . It is surprising that criticism should have hitherto done so little justice to [it]. . . . When *The Last Man* is reprinted it will come before the world as a new work.[1]

And the writers of our own century, with two prominent exceptions,[2] have continued this note of praise and this imputation of neglect. In 1938, R. Glynn Grylls claimed that "*The Last Man . . .* has not received its deserts."[3] In 1951, Muriel Spark, in a book published at the centenary of Mary Shelley's death, lamented that "her most interesting, if not her most consummate" novel was virtually inaccessible to readers; and she printed a thirty-five-page summary, interwoven with extensive quotations, as a partial substitute.[4] In 1953, Elizabeth Nitchie, writing from her unrivaled knowledge of Mary Shelley's entire work, argued that *The Last Man,* particularly in its latter sections where it achieves "an intensity of incident, scene, and feeling" that is often "impressive," deserves to be ranked as her best novel after *Frankenstein*—the last work of hers, in fact, in which Mary "allowed her imagination to play freely with the wonderful and the strange."[5]

As a result, the appearance of a scholarly reprinting of *The Last Man* in 1965 seemed, at the least, a justifiable addition to the list of nineteenth-century works now being made more readily available.[6] J. M. S. Tompkins, for example, in the *Keats-Shelley Journal,* greeted the reissue with the remark that "this is a timely and well-edited reprint of a faulty but interesting and, at times, impressive book."[7] Another reviewer, writing in a magazine of general rather than scholarly appeal, found that in many ways *The Last Man* revealed more about the Romantic period than did *Frankenstein* and that its reappearance "must be welcomed."[8] Ernest Lovell, Jr., himself the author of two shrewd, persuasive articles on the Byronic image in Mary Shelley's novels, remarked in a brief review that *"The Last Man* [is] equal in many ways to Mary's *Frankenstein* [and] is well worth reprinting."[9]

Clearly, then, *The Last Man* deserves serious attention in any assessment of Mary Shelley's career. Indeed, although the novel is marred by overwriting and sentimentality (Mary's major literary vices) as well as by its excessive length, *The Last Man* is a book of genuine power. Less readable than *Valperga,* less intense and richly symbolic than *Frankenstein,* it easily surpasses, nonetheless, her three remaining novels and does seem, to me, to merit its current ranking of a firm second place (after *Frankenstein*) by virtue of a greater unity and a more substantial underlying conception than is found in *Valperga.* But, to understand all that Mary was doing in *The Last Man,* it is necessary to backtrack a little—back to July, 1822, in fact—before beginning a specific discussion of the novel.

I *Mary's Early Reaction to Shelley's Death*

"Conceive the terrible state in which the women are," Leigh Hunt wrote back to England on July 20, 1822, with the first news of the death of Shelley and Edward Williams.[10] And a "terrible state" it must have been, indeed. Trelawny, that most novelistic of biographers,[11] gives us some suggestion of what Mary and Jane Williams suffered during the long wait between the disappearance of the *Don Juan* on July 8 during a storm and the discovery more than a week later of the two decomposed bodies on the shores of the Mediterranean near Viareggio. Trelawny writes in his *Recollections,* describing his return on July 19 to the Casa Magni:

I went up the stairs, and, unannounced, entered the room. I neither spoke, nor did they question me. Mrs. Shelley's large gray eyes were fixed on my face. I turned away. Unable to bear this horrid silence, with a convulsive effort she exclaimed:

"Is there no hope?"

I did not answer, but left the room, and sent the servant with the children to them. The next day I prevailed on them to return with me to Pisa. The misery of that night and the journey of the next day, and of many days and nights that followed, I can neither describe nor forget.[12]

Whatever the deduction we may be tempted to make because of the considerable imaginative talent at work in this portrayal, Mary herself more than substantiates Trelawny's implications. Less than a month before Shelley's death, she had suffered a miscarriage that was nearly fatal; and the blow of her husband's loss, we do well to remember, fell on an already physically depleted woman. "Both Lord Byron and [the Countess Guiccioli] have told me since," Mary wrote to Maria Gisborne, in a description of what her condition had been on July 12, when she and Jane Williams had arrived at Pisa still hoping desperately for good news,

that on that terrific evening I looked more like a ghost than a woman— light seemed to emanate from my features, my face was very white, I looked like marble—Alas. I had risen almost from a bed of sickness for this journey—I had travelled all day—it was now twelve at night—& we, refusing to rest, proceeded to Leghorn—not in despair—no, for then we must have died; but with sufficient hope to keep up the agitation of spirits which was all my life.[13]

And at the end of August, in another letter to the same correspondent, Mary attempted to give some indication of what she had endured in the five weeks since she had learned of Shelley's death:

I shudder with horror when I look on what I have suffered; & when I think of the wild and miserable thoughts that have possessed me, I say to myself "Is it true that I ever felt thus?"—And then I weep in pity of myself. Yet each day adds to the stock of sorrow & death is the only end. I would study, & I hope I shall—I would write—& when I am settled I may—But were it not for the steady hope I entertain of joining him what a mockery all this would be. Without that hope I could not study or write, for fame and usefulness (except as far as regards my child) are nullities to me.[14]

Consequently, it would be a mistake to dismiss this tone—and there is a good deal more of the same to follow both in the letters and in the journal—as simply the indulgence of a morbid self-pity. Genuine physical weakness played its part in Mary's reaction to Shelley's death—genuine physical weakness and, what was far more important in her decision to write *The Last Man,* a painful sense of guilt.

For undoubtedly there is a sense of guilt in almost everything Mary wrote during the four or five months after Shelley's death. To confine ourselves for the moment to her letters, we detect again and again in them her conviction that she has injured Shelley. "One day I hope to be worthy to join him," she wrote to Medwin on July 29;[15] in late August, she told Maria Gisborne: "I have but one hope for which I live—to render myself worthy to join him";[16] and, in September, after she had moved to "hateful Genoa, where nothing speaks to me of him, except the sea, which is his murderer," she wrote to Claire that the thoughts aroused in her by studying Shelley's manuscripts "may render me . . . more worthy of him hereafter."[17] Indeed, this reiterated confession of unworthiness passes sometimes into the revulsion of a bitter self-contempt: "They are now about this fearful office [of burning Shelley's body]—& I live!"[18]

Nor is the cause for such guilt difficult to find, despite the cloak of mystification sometimes spread over the issue. Within a month after Shelley's death, Mary had written a long poem called "The Choice," in which she lamented how she had failed him while he was still alive:

> *Now fierce remorse and unreplying death*
> *Waken a chord within my heart, whose breath,*
> *Thrilling and keen, in accents audible*
> *A tale of unrequited love doth tell.*
> .   .   .
> *It speaks of cold neglect, averted eyes,*
> *That blindly crushed thy soul's fond sacrifice:—*
> *My heart was all thine own,—but yet a shell*
> *Closed in its core, which seemed impenetrable,*
> *Till sharp-toothed misery tore the husk in twain,*
> *Which gaping lies, nor may unite again.*
> *Forgive me! let thy love descend in dew*
> *Of soft repentance and regret most true.*[19]

This painful awareness on Mary's part that she had often disap-
pointed Shelley by her physical and emotional coldness to him is
well supported by other evidence. Jane Williams, in a letter of
1824 to Leigh Hunt, indicated "that the intercourse between Shelley
& Mary was not as happy as it should have been; and I remember
your telling me that our Shelley mentioned several circumstances
on that subject that distressed you during the short week you were
together and that you witnessed the pain he suffered on receiving
a letter from Mary at that period."[20] Shelley himself, in a letter
written only three weeks before his death, told John Gisborne of
his steadily increasing delight with Italy; but then he added: "I
only feel the want of those who can feel, and understand me.
Whether from proximity and the continuity of domestic intercourse, Mary does not."[21] Indeed, two years earlier, in a postscript
of his which has only recently come to light, Shelley gives us a
clear insight into one of Mary's major failings in "domestic intercourse"—her proneness to jealousy (not always unjustified)
and her irritability: "Clare is yet with us, and is reading Latin and
Spanish with great resolution. Poor thing! She is an excellent girl. . . .
Mary who, you know, is always wise, has been lately very good.
I wish she were as wise now as she will be at 45, or as misfortune
has made me. She would then live on very good terms with Clare. . . .
Of course you will not suppose that Mary has seen . . . this . . .
so take no notice of it in any letter intended for her inspection."[22]
Years later, when she was busy composing a series of biographical
sketches for Lardner's *Cabinet Cyclopedia,* Mary apparently
attempted to justify to herself this failing in her personality. Writing
of the character of Voltaire's mistress, Madame du Châtelet,
Mary observed: "She has several of the faults attributed to literary
women, which arise from their not having the physical strength
to go through great intellectual labour without suffering from
nervous irritation."[23]

But it is in Shelley's poetry and in Mary's reaction to it that
we perhaps find the surest basis for believing that her sense of
guilt has something more to it than a purely imaginary foundation.
In "Epipsychidion," for example, to take only the most signal
instance, Shelley likens Mary to "the Moon," to "The chaste cold
Moon" (l. 281), with whom he is condemned to lie "within a chaste
cold bed" (l. 299)—an accusatory analogy which struck Mary as
so painfully just that she recurred to it after Shelley's death not

only in the privacy of her journal but also in the relative openness of her correspondence, when she asked Byron rhetorically, after having mentioned her eight years of "happiness" with Shelley, "Where also is he, who gone has made this quite, quite another earth from that which it was?—There might be [*sic*] something sunny about me then, now I am truly *cold moonshine*."[24] And on October 5, 1822, when Mary was planning for at least the second time to begin a biography of Shelley, she referred once more to the justice of the analogy in "Epipsychidion": "Well, I shall commence my task," she wrote in her journal; "commemorate the virtues of the only creature worth loving or living for, and then, maybe, I may join him. Moonshine may be united to her planet and wander no more, a sad reflection of all she loved on earth."[25]

Furthermore, this last reference is of value because it points clearly to Mary's instinctive methods of cushioning the shock of her remorse. For, if she ached under the dread that she had failed Shelley while he was alive, her most obvious resource was to make every restitution that she could to the eidolon of his memory. Easiest of all, of course, was to deify him in her own private musings. And so, in a fragment written apparently sometime in the autumn of 1822, we find Mary declaring: "I was the chosen mate of a celestial spirit. He has left me, and I am here to learn wisdom until I am fitted to join him in his native sky."[26] Again, in an apostrophe she confided to her journal on November 10, 1822, Mary wrote: "Mine own Shelley! the sun knows of none to be likened to you— brave, wise, gentle, noble-hearted, full of learning, tolerance, and love. Love! what a word for me to write! Yet, my miserable heart, permit me yet to love—to see him in beauty, to feel him in beauty, to be interpenetrated by the sense of his excellence; and thus to love, singly, eternally, ardently, and not fruitlessly; for I am still his—still the chosen one of that blessed spirit—still vowed to him for ever and ever!"[27]

Moreover, in addition to this instinctive attempt to turn Shelley into a demi-god within her own mind—and we would be foolish to underestimate the effect such an effort must have had on Mary's later, ambivalent, often embittered widowhood—Mary also assumed the heavy responsibility of righting Shelley's account with a public that had largely condemned or ignored him during his lifetime. Thus, as early as August, 1822, she wrote to Maria Gisborne: "I can conceive but of one circumstance that could afford

me the semblance of content—that is the being permitted to live
where I am now [in Italy] in the same house, in the same state,
occupied alone with my child in collecting His manuscripts—
writing his life, and thus to go easily to my grave."[28] And four
months later, on December 19, Mary prepared herself once more
for the act that was clearly going to constitute her fullest restitution
to Shelley's memory—the writing of his life. "And you, my own
Boy!" she wrote to her son in the privacy of her journal. "I am
about to begin a task, which if you live will be an invaluable treasure
to you in after times. I must collect my materials, & then, in the
commemoration of the divine virtues of your father, I shall fulfill
the only act of pleasure there remains to me."[29]

But, of course, Mary was never to write Shelley's biography;
and it is here, in the interconnection between her desire to "commemorate" Shelley's memory and her failure to do so in any formal
fashion, that we find a central importance for an understanding
of *The Last Man.* For, although Mary had employed various
aspects of Shelley in her fictional creations while he was still alive
(most notably in the Woodville of *Mathilda* and in the Euthanasia
of *Valperga*), she produced in *The Last Man* the only acknowledged
portrait of Shelley in all her fiction: the character of Adrian, the
second Earl of Windsor. "I was more aware than any other of his
wondrous excellencies," Mary wrote to John Bowring in February,
1826, shortly after *The Last Man* had been published, "& . . . I
have endeavoured, but how inadequately, to give some idea of him
in my last published book—the sketch has pleased some of those
who best loved him."[30] And Thomas Jefferson Hogg, surely one
of "those who best loved" Shelley, confirms our reading of Mary's
intention in her third novel by writing back to her on March 22:
"I read your *Last Man* with an intense interest and not without
tears. . . . The character of Adrian is most happy and just."[31]
In short, through the character of Adrian, Mary is undoubtedly
attempting to present an image of the idealized Shelley that her
conscience demanded she present.

But it also seems highly suggestive that the closest Mary could
come in these years to a biography of Shelley was in the fictionalized
portrait she offered in *The Last Man.* In 1822, as we have seen,
she mentioned her plan for writing Shelley's life as early as August;
and she apparently made an effort to begin to do so on at least
three separate occasions that year—on October 5, on November 11,

and on December 19. In early 1823 she made three more efforts—on February 10, on March 2, and on March 25.[32] Yet so far as we know, she was able to achieve from these beginnings only a total of eleven pages of fragments. Furthermore, in September, 1823, when she was specifically asked to write a biographical notice of Shelley for her edition of the *Posthumous Poems,* she declined the task and requested Leigh Hunt to do it for her instead.[33]

Such a refusal, of course, could have grown out of any number of reasons—physical weariness, a reluctance to relive the anguish of Shelley's loss, or even a dread of dwelling on those moments when she had been happier. Yet, in conjunction with the fact that Mary had apparently started a biography of Shelley on at least six different occasions in 1822–23 and had achieved only a total of eleven pages, it seems likely that a far more significant reason existed than any of those I have named above: on some instinctive level Mary must have been aware of a profound contradiction in her own attitude toward Shelley. On the one hand, of course, he was that ethereal figure of perfection that her imagination and her lacerated conscience so deeply needed to create; on the other, as a woman of Mary's intelligence could not help knowing, Shelley was that frightening figure of self-will who had made both his own father and Mary's apprehensive at the prospect of what he might do if he were balked; who could write a series of brutally self-justified letters to his pregnant first wife after he had eloped with Mary; who could continue a flirtatious interlude with Claire while Mary herself suffered through a difficult pregnancy and the ensuing miseries of the loss of her first child; who could state with a perfect sincerity that is almost chilling in its revelation of egoistic complacency: "I always go on until I am stopped, and I never am stopped." The reason Mary could never really begin a biography of Shelley in the months and years after his death, then, was that she probably could not allow the profound conflict in her attitude to his memory to rise into full consciousness: as she must have known intuitively, the "celestial Spirit" and the actual man were hopelessly incompatible.[34]

And it also seems likely that this ambivalent attitude of Mary's toward Shelley's memory played an important part in the over-all implications of *The Last Man.* For in *The Last Man,* as I shall attempt to show later, we find Mary making an unconscious palinode to many of the political and social ideals she shared with

Shelley while he was still alive—ideals, furthermore, which she continued to share with his memory, although much less intensely, after *The Last Man* had been completed. But, at this point, it is useful to examine briefly the history of the novel's composition and publication.

II *Composition and Publication*

Mary arrived in England on August 25, 1823, and soon began that curiously unintegrated life which Sylva Norman has described so accurately as the simultaneous existence of "the inconsolable recluse and the society widow."[35] By October 5, however, exactly one year after the journal entry in which she had announced she would "commemorate the virtues of the only creature worth loving or living for," Mary declared her intention of writing a novel that would, she told Leigh Hunt, be "wild & imaginative."[36] Four months later, on February 9, 1824, with her editing of Shelley's *Posthumous Poems* completed and with some minor articles out of the way, Mary decided "to plunge into a novel" in earnest, hoping "that its clear waters will wash off the mud of the magazines."[37] Although soon after this resolve she evidently passed through a period of deep creative doubt,[38] by May 14 she had decided on her title and was able to suggest, in a journal entry, the emotional and psychological atmosphere that permeates the latter stages of her book: "The last man! Yes, I may well describe that solitary being's feelings, feeling myself as the last relic of a beloved race, my companions extinct before me."[39]

But the following day, May 15, brought an unexpected shock and a subsequent interruption in composition; for on that date Mary learned of Byron's death at Missolonghi on April 19. In the privacy of her journal, she called on Byron's memory with the nickname the Shelleys had bestowed on him at Geneva: "Albe— the dear, capricious, fascinating Albe—has left this desert world! God grant I may die young! A new race is springing about me. At the age of twenty-six, I am in the condition of an aged person. All my old friends are gone. I have no wish to form new. I cling to the few remaining; but they slide away, and my heart fails when I think by how few ties I hold to the world."[40] Nor was Mary's reaction to Byron's death confined to her journal. Sometime within the next few months, it appears, she wrote an article in tribute to Byron's memory—an article which (aside from whatever problematic details in it entered the novel in the character of Raymond) is now unfortunately lost.[41]

But the shock of Byron's death must have been, on the whole, a salutary one for Mary; for it released her from the threat of the disturbing fascination she could not help feeling toward him, even when she was most mourning for Shelley's death.[42] And so in her next journal entry, we find Mary expressing a renewed sense of imaginative freedom:

> June 8.—What a divine night it is! I have just returned from Kentish Town; a calm twilight pervades the clear sky; the lamp-like moon is hung out in heaven, and the bright west retains the dye of sunset.
> If such weather would continue, I should write again; the lamp of thought is again illumined in my heart, and the fire descends from heaven that kindles it. . . . I feel my powers again, and this is, of itself, happiness; the eclipse of winter is passing from my mind. I shall again feel the enthusiastic glow of composition; again, as I pour forth my soul upon paper, feel the winged ideas arise, and enjoy the delight of expressing them.

Indeed, we are tempted to think that the memorial article on Byron was either fully conceived or actually written—and his living presence exorcised—in the interim between May 15 and June 8; for near the end of the journal entry of that date in June we find Mary addressing Shelley and telling him that, until tonight, "never was I so entirely yours."[43]

At any rate, whatever rush of composition followed the creative confidence expressed on June 8, we can hope for Mary's sake that it carried her through the summer of 1824. For, by September 3, she had recurred to the old note of despair and self-doubt:

> I have just completed my 27th year; at such a time hope and youth are still in their prime, and the pains I feel, therefore, are ever alive and vivid within me. What shall I do? Nothing! I study, that passes the time. I write, at times that pleases me; though double sorrow comes when I feel that Shelley no longer reads and approves of what I write; besides I have no great faith in my success. Composition is delightful, but if you do not expect the sympathy of your fellow creatures in what you write, the pleasure of writing is of short duration.[44]

And it seems likely that this tone of psychological isolation and creative malaise accompanied Mary during the remainder of her work on the novel, despite her often strenuous pursuit of her simultaneous career as "society widow."[45]

It was probably in the latter half of 1825 that composition ended, and publication itself took place in February of the following year. For her work the firm of Henry Colburn had paid Mary three hundred pounds, a sum which impressed Thomas Jefferson Hogg as quite generous.[46] Unfortunately, the reviewers of *The Last Man* were neither impressed nor generous. *Blackwood's,* which had been more than kind to both *Frankenstein* and *Valperga,* complained of the "stupid cruelties" in Mary's third novel.[47] For the *London Magazine, The Last Man* was "an elaborate piece of gloomy folly." The *Monthly Review* claimed that the novel could only be the product of mental unbalance. And, to rub salt into the wound of a lacerated ego, Sir Timothy Shelley became outraged at the Shelley name's being bandied about in insulting reviews and promptly threatened Mary with the loss of the small allowance he had granted her.[48] Altogether, *The Last Man* was hardly a glorious finale to Mary's career as a novelist. For, although she was to write three more extended works of fiction, their literary interest, while perhaps somewhat underrated, is in all truth close to negligible in comparison to the fascination the works possess as potential hunting grounds for the biographers of Mary and Shelley.

III *The Novel*

Perhaps the first point to be made about *The Last Man* is that in its overt subject—the destruction of mankind—Mary has adopted a fashionable theme of early nineteenth-century literature. Possibly, as Sylva Norman suggests, this widespread interest was initiated by an anonymous novel of 1806, *The Last Man, or Omegarus and Syderia.*[49] But, in any case, by 1816, Byron had written his "Darkness"; by 1824, Thomas Campbell had published his own "Last Man"; and, by 1826, Thomas Hood had published still another poem with the same title. Of all the treatments of this common theme, Mary's novel is by far the longest and the most interesting.

It opens, not with the story proper, but with the curious, rather illogical Author's Introduction. In it, in a partial return to the strategy of *Frankenstein*—that is, to the authenticating of the unnatural by a natural opening—we are told that the novel is really the product of editorial labors. The story which follows has been deciphered and pieced together from the inscriptions (in various languages) found on scattered leaves and bark in the Sibyl's Cave at Baiae, near Naples. (Mary and Shelley visited Baiae on December 8, 1818, a trip made memorable both by Shelley's letters and by his "Ode to the West Wind.") The illogicality of the introduction consists in a paradoxical undercutting of the authenticating intent: for, if the author of the inscriptions truly is the "last man" of a devastated world, as the novel presents him, then the supposed finding of his written record long afterward is an obvious, unauthenticating stroke.

Told in the first person by Lionel Verney, *The Last Man* is set in a period of futurity, the latter part of the twenty-first century. Lionel is the child of a former favorite of the last king of England, who, abdicating in 2073 and assuming the title of Earl of Windsor, voluntarily permitted England to become a republic. Lionel's father, however, had alienated the king well before the abdication by his reckless and dissolute behavior, so that, dismissed from the court and condemned by debts to drift into obscurity, he takes up residence in the Lake country. There, falling ill, he makes acquaintance with the daughter of a poor cottager, is nursed by her, and eventually marries her. From this union, first Lionel (whose birth seems to fall in the year 2063, ten years before the abdication of the king) and then Perdita, a girl three years younger than Lionel, are born. When Lionel is five, the two children are orphaned; and, from the lack of any firm guidance or parental love, Lionel soon grows into a rude savage. What saves him from utter worthlessness is his meeting at the age of sixteen with Adrian, the second Earl of Windsor, son of the (now deceased) last king of England. Adrian's generosity and sweetness of manner, his deep learning, and his passionate belief in the power of love and wisdom quickly effect a moral transformation in Lionel. " 'This,' I thought, 'is power! Not to be strong of limb, hard of heart, ferocious, and daring; but kind, compassionate and soft" (19).

Soon after this friendship has been formed, three other important characters are introduced: Evadne, daughter of the Greek ambassador to England; Idris, Adrian's sister; and Lord Raymond, who has already achieved military glory in Greece. A romantic sextet begins, the finale of which is to link Raymond with Perdita and Lionel with Idris, leaving two of the earlier players (Adrian vainly in love with Evadne, and Evadne vainly in love with Raymond) standing to one side, watching the newly formed quartet play on.

But well before this point, fortunately—for it is certainly not in this plot that the strength of *The Last Man* resides—political issues have deepened the implications of the novel. Raymond desires "to attain the first station in his own country" (27)—that is, to pursue the path which will eventually restore, in his own person, the monarchy of England. At first, his strongest opposition springs from Ryland, an adversary who clearly represents, in his over-all presentation, both the virtues and the limitations of the kind of mind (William Cobbet's?)[50] which Mary thought likely to come into prominence in a republic. For Ryland, although he is sincere in his championing of individual liberty and the continuance of the republic, is himself a mediocre man, severely handicapped by his moral and philosophical ignorance. (It can hardly be an accidental point that Ryland, when he finally does become Lord Protector after Raymond's resignation, shows himself to be utterly unworthy of responsibility; for he resigns the protectorship to Adrian in a fit of terror at the approaching plague.)

At this early stage of the novel, however, Ryland is able to deflect Raymond's royalist purposes far less than is Raymond himself. In an interesting reexamination of the basic conflict of *Valperga,* Mary now presents Raymond as torn, like Castruccio, between the desire for political power and the demands of his emotional nature. On the one hand, it will be most politic for Raymond to ally himself in marriage with Idris, Adrian's sister, and the daughter of the late king. On the other hand, Raymond is in love with Perdita, Lionel's sister, who is, of course, an obscure commoner. And, in *The Last Man,* Raymond reverses Castruccio's decision; he chooses to follow love instead of ambition.

But marriage with Perdita does not, as Mary implies in *Valperga* that Castruccio's true marriage with Euthanasia would, resolve the conflict. For Raymond simply has too much energy and too great a desire for prominence to remain content within the confines of domesticity. "My dear Lionel," Raymond says soon after his marriage to Perdita, in a mixture of self-delusion and self-scorn, "*we* are married men, and find employment sufficient in amusing our wives, and dancing our children. But Adrian is alone, wifeless, childless, unoccupied. . . . He pines for want of some interest in life" (67). That is, through Raymond's obvious projection of his own dissatisfaction onto Adrian, Mary explores the suggested solution of *Valperga*—and, indeed, by anticipation explores the actual "solution" of Victorian England—and finds it wanting: domesticity is not enough to contain the psychic energies of the aspiring mind.

Thus Raymond moves back into politics, swiftly gains the lord protectorship, still has Perdita as a loving wife—and discovers that even so much is not enough. When Evadne drifts into his life again, he finds himself drawn to her, wrecks his domestic life, and resigns the lord protectorship in bitter anger at his inability to function as an integrated human being. "I cannot rule myself," he tells Adrian when the latter tries to restrain him from giving up his high office:

My passions are my masters; my smallest impulse my tyrant. Do you think that I renounced the Protectorate . . . in a fit of spleen? By the God that lives, I swear never to take up that bauble again; never again to burthen myself with the weight of care and misery, of which that is the visible sign.

Once I desired to be a king. It was in the hey-day of my youth, in the pride of boyish folly. I knew myself when I renounced it. I renounced it to gain—no matter what—for that also I have lost. For many months I have submitted to this mock majesty—this solemn jest. I am its dupe no longer. I will be free. (109–10)

Determined to resume his military career, Raymond leaves England for Greece.

Essentially, the first volume of *The Last Man* ends here. In the second volume, the scene shifts to Greece, where Lionel and Perdita travel in pursuit of Raymond, and then to Constantinople, where Raymond dies, the victim of an explosion as he enters the Turkish city. But, by this time, the plague has already made it appearance in the novel; and "death had become lord of Constantinople" (139). The remainder of the second volume and all of the third deal with the inexorable advance of the plague over the inhabited portions of the globe until, as the desperate and distracted remnants of the world's population wander helplessly across Europe, only eighty survivors are left at Dijon; fifty, at the foot of the Jura Mountains; four, near the sources of the Arveiron River; and, finally, in the closing pages, three, at Como: Adrian, Clara (the orphaned daughter of Raymond and Perdita), and Lionel. Although at this point the virulence of the plague has so exhausted itself that it is no longer a threat to life, Lionel is not to be spared the anguish of a complete and irrevocable isolation: in a boat with Clara and Adrian on their voyage to Greece, a storm bears down on them, the boat is overturned, Clara and Adrian drown, and Lionel is left alone. The last human being in the world, he is condemned to linger out his years without hope of companionship or social intercourse. As a partial palliative to his hopeless isolation, he decides to write the history of "Verney—the LAST MAN." And on this note the novel ends.

IV *General Implications*

From such a summary it is easy enough to find Mary's psychological condition of isolation mirrored in her third novel. As the journal entry for May 14, 1824, clearly indicates, she must often have felt herself to be "the last relic of a beloved race" as she worked on the composition of *The Last Man*. Indeed, after taking up this clue and others, Muriel Spark has remarked: "Evidence of the physical analogy between the novel and its author occurs throughout; she depicted, in terms of enormously wide invention, the narrow and individual process which led to her own isolate situation in the years immediately following Shelley's death."[51] Elizabeth Nitchie, who has gone even farther than Muriel Spark, finds in the subject of *The Last Man* a reflection of Mary's most characteristic psychological trait: her sense of loneliness and isolation. "The theme of loneliness runs like a dark thread through much of her writing. . . . Through Mary's two best novels, *The Last Man* and *Frankenstein,* move two figures whose loneliness is final and irreparable."[52]

Although such criticism is helpful, it fails to take due note of a significant fact: that Mary Shelley, by virtue of her temperament and her experience, arrived at a psychic position which is strikingly similar to that reached by some of the greatest figures of the period. The similarity to Coleridge is perhaps most obvious since Mary felt a special affinity for *The Rime of the Ancient Mariner*. In her journal for April 16, 1841, for example, in the next to last entry of any substantive importance she was ever to make, Mary drew upon the Mariner's cry of anguish at his utter isolation and applied it to her own situation:

Alone—alone—all, all alone
Upon the wide, wide sea—
And God will not take pity on
My soul in agony![53]

In a letter of William Blake's of 1803 which Mary could not possibly have seen, we find this lament of the isolated sensibility:

O why was I born with a different face?
Why was I not born like the rest of my race?
When I look, each one starts! when I speak, I offend;
Then I'm silent & passive & lose every friend.

And in Wordsworth's poetry the note of isolation is so profound and persistent that A.C. Bradley has justly called him "the poet of solitude,"[54] and the more recent critic Herbert Lindenberger has been able to assert that "The central character throughout Wordsworth's work is the solitary. . . . Though Wordsworth was perhaps not entirely aware of it, the point in which the characters he chose to write about most resemble one another is their isolation—be it spiritual or physical—from any organized human context."[55] In short, in *The Last Man,* Mary Shelley, partly through the accident of temperament and experience, partly through the intention of design, undertook an artistic exploration of something far larger than a merely personal reaction to her own individual history.

Furthermore, the prevalence of the theme of a "last man" in the literature of the period also suggests that Mary had touched on something much richer than a drawn-out lament for her own emotional isolation. In truth, by connecting the two themes of the isolated sensibility and the death of civilization, Mary created a total effect that is remarkably prophetic of the paradox of modern industrial societies: as the extension of the suffrage and the diffusion of wealth have tended to dissolve the older hierarchies of class, the isolation of the creative (as opposed to the mechanical) personality has tended to become more and more pronounced; and a chronic voice of fear continues to make itself heard that the most prized values of civilized existence are scarcely viable any longer.

Moreover, if Mary's novel can be said to look ahead into the

later nineteenth century and on into the twentieth, it also surely
looks back—back to Pope's great and intensely pessimistic vision
of the future of modern civilization (the probable true source of
Byron's "Darkness"):

> *She comes! she comes! the sable throne behold*
> *Of* Night *primeval, and of Chaos old!*
>
> .   .   .
>
> *Thus at her felt approach, and secret might,*
> Art *after* art *goes out, and all is Night.*
>
> .   .   .
>
> Religion *blushing veils her sacred fires,*
> *And unawares* Morality *expires.*
> *For* public *flame, nor* private, *dares to shine;*
> *Nor* human *spark is left, nor glimpse* divine!
> *Lo! thy dread empire,* CHAOS! *is restored;*
> *Light dies before thy uncreating word:*
> *Thy hand, great Anarch! lets the curtain fall;*
> *And universal darkness buries All.*

(The Dunciad, IV. 629–56)

For, although Pope's lines were written almost a century earlier
than Mary's novel, *The Last Man* does reflect (at times confusedly)
that same spirit of conservation and dread of excessive change that
we have already noted in the surface implications of *Frankenstein.*
Indeed, in the novel's combination of prophetic elements of total
disaster with retrospective glimpses of the superiority of the firmer
hierarchies of the past, we find an interesting similarity to the literary sensibilities of our own century—those, for example, of William
Butler Yeats, T.S. Eliot, F.R. Leavis—who have been most
pessimistic about the nature of industrial democracy. At this point,
however, a closer look at the novel is necessary to make these
contentions clear.

V *The Plague as Symbol*

For the most part, the suggestive structure of *The Last Man*
appears to have been misunderstood. Because more than a third
of the novel deals not with the plague at all but with political and
romantic elements in republican England, a common criticism is
that Mary has provided an unduly tedious introduction to the "real"

theme of her book—the plague itself and its far-reaching consequences. Yet such a charge—despite the undoubted tedium of some
of the passages dealing with the love relationships—fails to take
note of the full implications of *The Last Man*. For, in its deepest
import, the novel achieves a striking fusion of the theme of the
plague (in the second and third volumes) with the theme of political
and social change implicit from the outset in the presentation of
England as a republic. Indeed, Mary, who quotes approvingly
from Burke's *Reflections on the French Revolution* at least twice
in the course of her novel (165, 300), has produced in *The Last Man*
a pervasive criticism of her father's (and, to a degree, of Shelley's)
theory of society—a criticism of which Burke himself would have
approved.

In Chapter 4 of the first volume, for example, Ryland appears on
the scene as the chief opponent of Raymond's early bid for political power. Fully aware that Raymond wishes to overturn the republic
and become king, Ryland rises to confront him with a speech that
seems to reflect the triumph of many of the ideas advanced by Shelley
in his "Philosophical View of Reform":

> Ryland began by praising the present state of the British empire. He
> recalled past years to their memory; the miserable contentions which in
> the time of our fathers arose almost to civil war, the abdication of the late
> king, and the foundation of the republic. He described this republic;
> shewed how it gave privilege to each individual in the state, to rise to con-
> sequence, and even to temporary sovereignty. He compared the royal and
> republican spirit; shewed how the one tended to enslave the minds of men;
> while all the institutions of the other served to raise even the meanest
> among us to something great and good. He shewed how England had
> become powerful, and its inhabitants valiant and wise, by means of the
> freedom they enjoyed. (41–42)

Yet this presentation of Ryland as the apparent champion of
many of Shelley's most prominent political ideas[56] becomes
immeasurably more complex in the second volume, once the theme
of the plague has been announced. For Ryland, now that Raymond
is dead, stands on the very threshold of political power himself;
and the policy he intends to pursue if elected lord protector is
clearly that of the extension of Shelley's "divine Equality": "The
political state of England became agitated as the time drew near
when the new Protector was to be elected. This event excited the

more interest, since it was the current report that if the popular candidate (Ryland) should be chosen, the question of the abolition of hereditary rank, and other feudal relics, would come under the consideration of parliament" (160).

To Burke, of course, such a proposal as the one attributed to Ryland would have seemed a threat to the very principle of social order. "The power of perpetuating our property in our families," Burke declares in his *Reflections,* "is one of the most valuable . . . circumstances belonging to it, and that which tends the most to the perpetuation of society itself. . . . The possessors of family wealth, and of the distinction which attends hereditary possession . . . are the natural securities for this transmission."[57] And again, in a claim that clearly associates the continuation of what we would today call "culture"[58] with a continuation of the system that Ryland intends to overturn, Burke asserts: "Nothing is more certain, than that our manners, our civilization, and all the good things which are connected with manners, and with civilization, have, in this European world of ours, depended for ages upon two principles; and were indeed the result of both combined; I mean the spirit of a gentleman and the spirit of religion."[59]

Nor is this analogue an idle one, for Burke's argument becomes a part of the texture of Mary's novel as she presents the entire English nation as considering the abolition of rank and title: "The newspapers teemed with nothing else; and in private companies the conversation, however remotely begun, soon verged towards this central point, while voices were lowered and chairs drawn closer. The nobles did not hesitate to express their fear; the other party [that is, the "popular" party] endeavoured to treat the matter lightly" (161). Thus Ryland attempts to dismiss the whole storm of fear and uncertainty with the supremely self-confident rationality of a Jeremy Bentham—or of a William Godwin: " 'Shame on the country,' said Ryland, 'to lay so much stress upon words and frippery; it is a question of nothing; of, the new painting of carriage-panels and the embroidery of footmen's coats' " (161).

Yet immediately after this bluff dismissal of aristocratic objections, a long paragraph follows on the prospect of an egalitarian society, a paragraph which presents, ostensibly through Lionel's reflections, the major arguments for and against such an innovation. First, there is the popular party's glowing prediction of what will actually occur in England, despite the widespread fear in the nation that a "democratic style" may introduce a change for the worse:

Yet could England indeed doff her lordly trappings, and be content with the democratic style of America? Were the pride of ancestry, the patrician spirit, the gentle courtesies and refined pursuits, splendid attributes of rank, to be erased among us? We were told that this would not be the case. ... We were assured that, when the name and title of Englishman was the sole patent of nobility, we should all be noble; that when no man born under English sway, felt another his superior in rank, courtesy and refinement would become the birth-right of all our countrymen. (161)

But second, and of course counter to this egalitarian argument, runs the Burkean claim of the aristocratic party, which contends that in truth the highest achievements of civilization are at stake: "That party ... could hardly yet be considered a minority in the kingdom, who extolled the ornament of the column, 'the Corinthian capital of polished society'; they appealed to prejudices without number, to old attachments and young hopes; to the expectation of thousands who might one day become peers; they set up as a scarecrow, the spectre of all that was sordid, mechanic and base in the commercial republic" (161).

And then, with the opening words of the next paragraph, Mary fuses her two themes. "The plague had come to Athens," she writes starkly, exactly as, in the opening sentence of the paragraph directly preceding her description of the egalitarian conflict in England, she had written: "But, though it seemed absurd to calculate upon the arrival of the plague in London, I could not reflect without extreme pain on the desolation this evil would cause in Greece" (160). For, to put it as simply as possible, Mary Shelley, on the deepest symbolic level, surely unaware herself of the full implications of her novel, has created a startlingly pessimistic allegory which identifies egalitarianism with a plague virulent enough to destroy civilization itself.

Nor is this reading in the least a fanciful one. In *Valperga,* Mary made a similar identification, although there, with Shelley still alive, she projected her deepest fears (and they are close to Burke's) onto one of Castruccio's dark angels, Galeazzo Visconti. "The contagion of liberty is dangerous," Galeazzo tells Castruccio: "the Ghibellines [the royalist party] must fall in Lucca, if the Guelphs [the republican party] be not destroyed in Florence. Think you, if your people are allowed free intercourse with this republic, that the plague of liberty will not spread to your state? For no quarantine will eradicate that spot, if once it has entered the soul" (II, 12).

In *The Last Man,* however, Mary Shelley, despondent, psychologically isolated, bitterly resentful over the lack of charity in ordinary humanity (Sir Timothy's harshness and an apparent series of social snubs led her into a misanthropic entry in her journal on December 3, 1842),[60] produced a novel in which her fears are no longer projected by a minor figure but are incorporated into the very texture of her work.

Symbolically, then, the true subject of *The Last Man* is "the plague of liberty" and its egalitarian consequences. The first volume, with its political concerns, introduces us to an England where the old hierarchies (the monarchy in particular) have broken down; and then, as the novel progresses through its second and third volume, we are presented with the horrified vision of a world from which all social distinctions have vanished and where every man is reduced to the lowest common denominator—that of his most primitive animal interests.

"The race of man had lost in fact all distinctions of rank," we are told as the plague continues to rage across England. And a passage soon follows that reveals the catastrophe such egalitarianism brings to the fabric of society and to the genuine dignity of man:

There was but one good and one evil in the world—life and death. The pomp of rank, the assumption of power, the possessions of wealth vanished like morning mist. One living beggar had become of more worth than a national peerage of dead lords—alas the day! than of dead heroes, patriots, or men of genius. There was much of degradation in this: for even vice and virtue had lost their attributes—life—life—the continuation of our animal mechanism—was the Alpha and Omega of the desires, the prayers, the prostrate ambition of [the] human race. (212)

Furthermore, with the abandonment of hard and fast hierarchies of labor, the scale of civilized values is reversed, and the most menial abilities rise to the ascendancy:

Without the aid of servants, it was necessary to discharge all household duties; hands unused to such labour must knead the bread, or in the absence of flour, the statesmen [sic] or perfumed courtier must undertake the butcher's office. Poor and rich were now equal, or rather the poor were the superior, since they entered on such tasks with alacrity and experience; while ignorance, inaptitude, and habits of repose, rendered them fatiguing to the luxurious, galling to the proud, disgusting to all whose minds, bent on intellectual improvement, held it their dearest privilege to be exempt from attending to mere animal wants. (223)

And this fusion of the ravages of the plague with the destructive consequences of a thoroughgoing social equality is heightened into genuine, almost Burkean intensity in the opening pages of the third volume. With a nostalgic look backward at a God-centered world, where, paradoxically, man's stature was enlarged through his acceptance of the principle of subordination, Mary writes:

Once man was a favourite of the Creator, as the royal psalmist sang, "God had made him a little lower than the angels, and had crowned him with glory and honour." . . . Once it was so; now is man lord of the creation? Look at him—ha! I see plague! She has invested his form, is incarnate in his flesh, has entwined herself with his being, and blinds his heaven-seeking eyes. Lie down, O man, on the flower-strown earth; give up all claim to your inheritance, all you can ever possess of it is the small cell which the dead require. (229–30)

For now that all men are reduced to the lowest common denominator, heroic effort is a thing of the past; and intellectual distinction has dwindled to a low cunning that is useful for nothing more than the preservation of life:

Plague is the companion of spring, of sunshine, and plenty. We no longer struggle with her. We have forgotten what we did when she was not. Of old navies used to stem the giant ocean-waves betwixt Indus and the Pole for slight articles of luxury. Men made perilous journies to possess themselves of earth's splendid trifles, gems and gold. Human labour was wasted—human life set at nought. Now life is all that we covet; that this automaton of flesh should, with joints and strings in order, perform its functions, that this dwelling of the soul should be capable of containing its dweller. Our minds, late spread abroad through countless spheres and endless combinations of thought, now retrenched themselves behind this wall of flesh, eager to preserve its well-being only. We were surely sufficiently degraded. (230)

And this overture to the third volume ends with a dying fall that is a palinode to the liberal hopes of an age—a palinode, it must be added, to many of the liberal hopes that Mary herself, on the conscious level of her mind, was to continue to hold almost until her death:

As the rules of order and pressure of laws were lost, some began with hesitation and wonder to transgress the accustomed uses of society. Palaces were deserted, and the poor man dared at length, unreproved, intrude into the splended apartments, whose very furniture and decorations were an unknown world to him. . . . We were all equal now; magnificent dwellings, luxurious carpets, and beds of down, were afforded to all. Carriages and horses, gardens, pictures, statues, and princely libraries, there were enough of these even to superfluity; and there was nothing to prevent each from assuming possession of his share. We were all equal now; but near at hand was an equality still more levelling, a state where beauty and strength, and wisdom, would be as vain as riches and birth. (230–31)

For it was only in the last years of her life, as she watched with horror the revolutions of 1848, that Mary allowed into full consciousness the Burkean fears that were hers in 1824–25 during the composition of *The Last Man*. "Strange & fearful events are in progress in Europe," she wrote on June 30, 1848. "Barbarism—countless uncivilized men, long concealed under the varnish of our social system, are breaking out with the force of a volcano & threatening order—law & peace. In Germany the bands of society are entirely broken—no rents are paid—the peasant invades the Chateau— & would take it—were it worth his while."[61] But, as I have tried to show, this horrified reaction of 1848 is only the waking counterpart to the powerful and extended nightmare of *The Last Man,* a nightmare whose deepest symbolic import was concealed from even Mary herself.

VI *The Paradox of Mary's Novel*

Yet the question remains as to what was the real cause behind Mary's writing so pessimistic a novel on the future of the democratic ideal—especially when, as we have seen, she explicitly intended to memorialize Shelley in the character of Adrian? In addition to this problem how are we to reconcile her later statements which reflect a liberal sentiment with the undoubtedly conservative implications of her third novel? In 1838, for example, in her biographic sketch of Montaigne, she criticizes him for his dislike of reformers; and she supports, unequivocally, the principle implicit in the French Revolution: "This [that is, Montaigne's dislike of reformers] is no lofty view of the great and holy work of reformation, the greatest and (however stained by crime, the effect of the most cruel persecutions) the most beneficent change operated in modern times in human institutions."[62] Again, in 1839, Mary wrote of the "evil counsellors" who selfishly advised Louis against yielding to the spirit of reform in 1789.[63] Perhaps most important, since it touches on the very fears implicit in *The Last Man,* is the following statement of Mary's which appeared in 1844 in the last book she was to publish, *Rambles in Germany and Italy:*

> The blessing which the world now needs is the steady progress of civilization: freedom, by degrees, it will have, I believe. Meanwhile, as the fruits of liberty, we wish to perceive the tendency of the low to rise to the level of the high—not the high to be dragged down to the low. This, we are told by many, is the inevitable tendency of equality of means and privileges. I will hope not: for on that hope is built every endeavour to banish ignorance, and hard labour and penury, from political society.[64]

"I will hope not. . . ." Surely with such a sentiment, in its brave generosity and cautious faith, we are brought back to our critical problem: how can we explain the deep contradiction between the implications of Mary's third novel and the often liberal ideas she expressed in the years after it—almost, in fact, until her death in 1851?

A part of our solution, no doubt, lies in Mary's personal situation during the composition of *The Last Man.* As I have already indicated, her emotional condition was such that she had to contend against her feelings of deep bitterness toward the common run of humanity; for she wrote in her journal on December 3, 1824: "The struggle is hard that can give rise to misanthropy in one, like me, attached to my fellow-creatures. Yet now, did not the memory of those matchless lost ones redeem their race, I should learn to hate men, who are strong only to oppress, moral only to insult."[65] Furthermore, the text itself confirms how sharply aware Mary was of human limitations as she worked on her novel. In Volume I, for example, Raymond is presented, like the Guinigi of *Valperga,* as a man who has surrendered his dream of military glory and is now working for the common good of society. Indeed, as Lord Protector of England, Raymond seems on the verge of finally establishing that ideal community which has tempted the political speculations of the most generous minds of Western civilization— including, of course, Shelley's own:

Meanwhile all went on well in London. . . . Raymond was occupied in a thousand beneficial schemes. Canals, aqueducts, bridges, stately buildings, and various edifices for public utility, were entered upon; he was continually surrounded by projectors and projects, which were to render England one scene of fertility and magnificence; the state of poverty was to be abolished. . . . The physical state of man would soon not yield to the beatitude of angels; disease was to be banished; labour lightened of its heaviest burden. (76)

But, as we know, Raymond fails in his pursuit of the utopian vision because of the limitations within his own nature. Torn in different directions by his emotions, he ends by bitterly resigning the protectorship, departs for Greece, and dies fighting for a liberty which, since the plague has already begun to reduce all men to complete equality, no longer possesses any meaning. The surest obstacle to utopia is the irrational element within humanity itself— an irrationality that is capable, contrary to all conscious decision, of driving the individual to his own destruction. (In this respect, at least, Mary's novel provides an anticipation of Dostoevski's *Notes from Underground:* man cannot bear, not too much reality, but too much rationality.)

But a second probable cause for the pessimistic quality of *The Last Man* can be found in the ambiguous nature of Mary's attitude to Shelley's memory. Quite clearly, her conscious intent of memorializing him in the character of Adrian was shot through with a resentment that insisted on cropping up in various parts of the novel. To take only the most obvious instance—although I believe it has not been noted before—Mary specifically refutes Shelley on the theory of love which he advanced in "Epipsychidion." In that poem, Shelley argues for the principle of free love with these lines:

> True Love in this differs from gold and clay,
> That to divide is not to take away.
>
> . . .
>
> If you divide suffering from dross, you may
> Diminish till it is consumed away;
> If you divide pleasure and love and thought,
> Each part exceeds the whole.
>
> (ll. 160–81)

In the novel, Mary passes this judgment on Raymond's dereliction from Perdita: "The affection and amity of a Raymond might be inestimable; but, beyond that affection, embosomed deeper than friendship was the indivisible treasure of love. Take the sum in its completeness, and no arithmetic can calculate its price; take from it the smallest portion, give it but the name of parts, separate it into degrees and sections, and like the magician's coin, the valueless gold of the mine, is turned to vilest substance" (93). Nor is this difference of opinion at all a trivial one, for "Epipsychidion" (along with the infatuation it recorded) was almost surely the most dangerous threat in the entire body of Shelley's poetry to Mary's memory of him as "a celestial spirit."

More than specific refutation, however, the very curve of Adrian's presentation seems to suggest a profound departure on Mary's part from certain of Shelley's ideas, regardless of how nobly generous and admirably courageous Adrian appears to be in the course of the novel. In an early description of Adrian's plans, for example, we are told of "his intention of using his influence to diminish the power of the aristocracy, to effect a greater equalization of wealth and privilege, and to introduce a perfect system of republican government into England" (30). But, if we reflect on this plan for a moment, we realize that it is virtually identical with the one Ryland attempts to put into practice shortly after Raymond's death. That is, what Mary has created is an implicit similarity between the idealism of Adrian and the pragmatism of Ryland. Moreover, this implicit similarity is intensified into an explicit stroke or ironic contrast as the plague moves nearer to Ryland's post of political power.

"Whither indeed would you fly? [Adrian asks the terrified Ryland.] We must all remain; and do our best to help our suffering fellow creatures."

"Help!" said Ryland, "there is no help!—great God, who talks of help! All the world has the plague!"

... Adrian paced the hall, revolving some new and powerful idea— suddenly he stopped and said: "I have long expected this; could we in reason expect that this island should be exempt from the universal visitation?... What are your plans, my Lord Protector, for the benefit of our country?"

"For heaven's love!..." cried Ryland, "do not mock me with that title. Death and disease level all men. I neither pretend to protect nor govern an hospital—such will England quickly become."...

"Faint-hearted man!" cried Adrian indignantly—"Your countrymen put their trust in you, and you betray them!"

"I betray them!" said Ryland, "the plague betrays me. . . . Take the
Protectorship who will; before God I renounce it!"
      "And before God," replied his opponent, fervently, "do I receive it!"
(175–77)

The deeper implication of this seems clear: Adrian, the Shelleyan
reformer, is finally granted political power in a universe where
death has become the measure of all things. The memorial to Shelley,
despite the good intentions of the sculptor, has a fairly obvious
(and perhaps irremediable) crack in its foundation.

      But, aside from the effects of a personal dejection and of a complex
reaction to Shelley's memory, a third reason lay behind the pessimistic implications of *The Last Man*. And in this third—and final—
reason we can perhaps discover a good deal of the explanation for
Mary Shelley's noticeable decline as a writer after her third novel.
That decline, of course, has been explained in various ways: by the
death of Shelley, which left Mary without the support and encouragement she so clearly required; by the need to make money with
her pen, which led her into an excessive concern to meet the popular
taste; by her own sense of social ambiguity during her long widowhood in England, which deprived her of any firm vantage point
for assessing experience. But, while all of these factors were no
doubt contributory to her creative deterioration, each one may
well be subsumed under a far more fundamental cause: that in
Mary Shelley the contradictions of the age were heightened to an
unusual degree within her own psychological makeup.

      Thus Muriel Spark has been able to write of Mary: "I do not
believe . . . that Mary ever . . . [became] wholly at one with the
currents of the Romantic revival. . . . To a great extent Mary
Shelley occupied an environment fifty years or more ahead of her."[66]
While Sylva Norman, with no less conviction (and accuracy), has
observed: "The sources of [Mary Shelley's] inspiration . . . are
those of the romantic—moonlight, trees and meadows, flowers
and sunshine. . . . And it is finally the romantic period that must be
borne in mind when we consider her, if we are not to confuse the
fashions of an age with the faults of an individual."[67] For neither
critic is really wrong. Mary Shelley actually did combine an instinctive commitment to the greater stability of the eighteenth
century along with a conscious espousal of much that was common
to early nineteenth-century individualism.

And in this respect, of course, she was—as Ernest Lovell, Jr., has pointed out—far closer in sympathy to Byron than to Shelley.[68] Indeed, her fundamental conflict between intellectual liberalism and constitutional conservatism probably explains the curious lack of reality in the social background of much of her fiction. As Sylva Norman has remarked: "For her characters, the rule of snobbery appeared to prevail; they must be highborn, whether they were the medieval chieftains of *Valperga,* the English princes of *Perkin Warbeck,* the society nobles of *Lodore* and *Falkner,* or the imaginary king's son of *The Last Man.*"[69]

Even more specifically, however, the deep-seated emotional reasons behind such a choice in characterization led Mary, in the first years of her widowhood, to write the novel that is most truly her own. Byron's presence at Geneva had aroused her to the depiction of Victor Frankenstein's defiance of human limitations; Shelley's intense political interests in Italy in 1819–20 had sparked the liberalism of *Valperga.* In *The Last Man,* however, alone in England with only a hopelessly idealized memory of Shelley, Mary allowed herself for once, despite her conscious intention of memorializing her husband, to pour into a work of fiction all her actual and profound social and political uncertainty about the future.

As a consequence, the fiction afterward seems so markedly inferior because it is undermined by a pervasive emotional and intellectual incoherence. On the one hand, there was the sincere dedication to Shelley and to much of what Mary believed Shelley had stood for (a dedication perhaps intensified by the attack of smallpox Mary suffered in 1828); on the other hand, there was the much greater conservatism of Mary's true nature. Out of such a split, unvivified by Shelley's actual presence, almost all of Mary's stories and her three remaining novels were written. And their unreality is announced on almost every page (*Perkin Warbeck* is a partial exception) by their repetitive sentimentality and by their consistent refusal to deal with the larger issues of the earlier novels—until at last, in 1848, with her creative impulses long a thing of the past, Mary breaks out anxiously to Alexander Berry:

These are awful times. The total overthrow of law, the dislocation of the social system in France presents a fearful aspect. In Italy & in Germany the people aim at political rather than social change—but the French will spare no pains to inculcate their wicked & desolating principles—&

to extend the power of their nefarious Provisional Government all over Europe. . . . There is no doubt that a French propaganda is spread among all the nations—they are rousing the Irish & even exciting the English Chartists. [70]

It is this same note—this same sensitivity to "the plague of liberty"— that is present (although controlled) in *Valperga* twenty-five years earlier and that is symbolically sustained throughout much of Mary's third, and perhaps most disturbing, novel, *The Last Man*.

CHAPTER 5

Other Fictional Prose and the Verse

A SIDE from her first three novels, little of Mary's fiction repays detailed attention. And this unhappy fact is perhaps even truer of her small body of poetry, including her two "little mythological dramas" (as their editor called them), *Proserpine* and *Midas*.[1] In this chapter, brief consideration is given to three broad areas of Mary's creative writing: (1) her three remaining novels; (2) her shorter fiction, including her *novella, Mathilda;* and (3) her verse.

I *The Three Remaining Novels*

A common misconception about Mary's three remaining novels— *The Fortunes of Perkin Warbeck* (1830), *Lodore* (1835), and *Falkner* (1837)—is that their inferiority is partly due to Mary's expending on them far less effort than she applied to her earlier fiction. However, two recently published letters of hers reveal beyond question how conscientiously she worked on the research and writing of *Perkin Warbeck*—first of all, going to a good deal of trouble to run down the most reliable historical sources available; and then, afterward, subjecting the original manuscript to a rigorous revision which reduced it in length by approximately 40 percent.[2] Furthermore, an unpublished journal entry for June 7, 1836, shows that Mary, while she was writing her last novel, *Falkner,* believed that it would be her best,[3] a sentiment which hardly suggests a diminished sense of dedication. For, although it is true that Mary did speak of *Lodore* as having been written "off hand,"[4] the evidence of her sustained effort on *Perkin Warbeck* and of her creative confidence in *Falkner* surely indicates a higher level of literary aspiration after Shelley's death than is usually recognized. And this, in its turn, seems to suggest what I have already argued in the preceding chapter: we must look elsewhere than to Mary's consciousness for an understanding of her decline.

Begun sometime before February 19, 1828,[5] and completed by January 1830,[6] *Perkin Warbeck* is easily the best of the three remaining novels. In many ways it resembles *Valperga,* not only because, like that novel, it has a historical setting, but also because it deals with the same essential subject: the conflict between political ambition and the desires of the human heart. Indeed, in Mary's choice of a protagonist—"Perkin," who is really Richard, the true king of England—she has given to her fourth novel a greater structural unity than *Valperga* possesses. And yet, despite this superior cohesiveness of plot, *Perkin Warbeck* is inferior to *Valperga* on at least two quite serious scores: it lacks, first of all, the vitality of characterization found in the earlier novel (Robin Clifford is perhaps a partial exception); and, second, the surface of its structural unity is undermined by an ideational incoherence in Richard (or "Perkin") which fails to create the tension that the earlier contradictions in *Frankenstein* and in *The Last Man* undoubtedly did. In short, *Perkin Warbeck* is essentially a lifeless novel, although it deserves our respect for the quality of the intelligence which is intermittently displayed in it.

The novel opens on August 22, 1485, at "the decisive battle of Bos-Worth Field";[7] and the death of Richard III and the triumph of Henry Richmond (soon to be crowned Henry VII) seem to promise some prospect of peace to an England distracted by prolonged internal disturbances between the rival factions of York and Lancaster. The defeated Yorkists, however, still harbor the hope of returning to power; and one of their leading adherents argues that "Richard IV" should be proclaimed at once—that is, that the young boy in hiding who is actually the son of the late Edward IV and the nephew of Richard III should be revealed immediately as the true successor to Richard III. (What Mary advances in her novel, then, is the theory that the boldest pretender to the throne during the reign of Henry VII—Perkin Warbeck— was in truth the legitimate king of England and not the imposter history has agreed to brand him.) But despite this rash suggestion that the boy be proclaimed king, more cautious counsels prevail; and Richard, the legitimate king of England, is spirited off to the Continent under his assumed name of Perkin Warbeck.

The remainder of the novel deals with this ambiguous role meted out to Richard. On the one hand, he carries with him the knowledge that he is the rightful king of England; on the other, he lacks both the certain power and the assured position which would ordinarily be his. Thus the conflict between his desire to become king in actuality and his own innate needs for the emotional satisfactions of ordinary humanity becomes an inevitable part of his characterization. At first because of his awareness of his eminence above others is dominant, he rejects the love of Monina, his childhood companion in obscurity, because she is a commoner; but then, with his marriage to Lady Katherine Gordon in Scotland, Richard comes to realize the primacy of the heart's emotions. For, after the failure of Richard's plan to dethrone Henry VII by an invasion from Scotland, Mary presents us with this analysis of his thoughts as he sails toward Ireland with Lady Katherine: "And Richard, marked for misery and defeat, acknowledged that power which sentiment possesses to exalt us—to convince us that our minds, endowed with a soaring, restless aspiration, can find no repose on earth except love" (III, 24–25).

Unfortunately, Richard, although he has come to realize the futility of his ambition, is driven on by his sense of honor. Because it is impossible for him to surrender the justice of his cause when so many faithful adherents have already suffered on his behalf, he continues his futile opposition to the much-too-wily Henry VII. Finally, because of the treachery of Robin Clifford, Richard is captured as he is about to board a ship which will carry him away from England. He is tried by Henry, convicted of treason and imposture, and executed in the year 1499. The novel then concludes with a brief description of Katherine's later years at the court of Henry VII—a description which sounds suspiciously like Mary's apologia for her own life in England after Shelley's death. For, in this brief conclusion, Katherine, who, we are assured, has remained absolutely faithful to the memory of her deceased husband, declares to a critic of her social life at court that isolation for her would be painfully unnatural: she cannot exist without the sympathy she finds in society (III, 354). Quite plainly, the "society widow" who doubled as "inconsolable recluse" was at least partly aware of the bizarre contradictions in her later life.[8]

But it is the ideational incoherence which exists in the character of Richard that invalidates much of the surface unity of *Perkin Warbeck*. That incoherence occurs because Richard, as the representative of an outmoded chivalry, is really an advocate of what we can only call "reactionary" policies. In wishing to turn the clock back on the world view which has triumphed on Bosworth Field, Richard fails to realize that the age of martial heroism is dead:

the grandeur of chivalry has been succeeded by the cunning policy-making of Henry VII. And yet, at the same time, Richard represents the insurrectionary tactics of a still later world view which eventually culminated (if it has culminated) in the French Revolution.[9] And, although this contradiction in Richard may well shed light on the hopeless split within Mary's own political and social views after Shelley's death, such a dichotomy within *Perkin Warbeck* almost completely deprives the novel of any genuine intellectual vitality. Richard simply becomes an impossibly absurd hero; caught between two worlds, he functions effectively in neither.

Furthermore, the over-all implication of the novel on its political and social level does seem quite revealing. Richard, as we have seen, is presented by Mary as the true king of England: noble, generous, and brave—an infinitely better man than Henry VII. Yet when Richard is attempting to increase his support in England, he is told by a former Yorkist: "My lord, I love not Tudor, but I love my country: and now that I see plenty and peace reign over this fair isle, even though Lancaster be the unworthy vicegerent [*sic*], shall I cast forth these friends of man to bring back the deadly horrors of unholy civil war?" (II, 147). That is, in terms of the ruinous consequences of Richard's hopes throughout the novel—the wasted lives, the despoiled homes, the internal unrest—this short passage of judgment leads to an unavoidable conclusion: the ultimate good of society depends far more on social stability than on any pursuit after abstract "justice." Like *The Last Man,* in other words, *Perkin Warbeck* is a novel of which Edmund Burke might conceivably approve.

Mary Shelley's next novel, *Lodore,* in its pervasive sentimentality, its absence of serious ideas, and its almost total lack of creative vitality, is the weakest of all her fiction; but, aside from *Frankenstein,* it is probably the one that has received the most attention from later readers of her work; for the biographers of Shelley have turned to the book as a promising source for filling in the lacunae of certain passages of their subject's life. Thus Edward Dowden, the first to recognize its concealed significance, wrote in 1886:

I may here point out . . . that some important passages of biography, transmuted for the purposes of fiction, may be found in Mrs. Shelley's novel *Lodore.* . . . In it . . . may be found an almost literal transcript from her life and that of Shelley during the weeks of distress and separation in London, which followed soon after their return from the Continent in 1814.

In it may be found in a transmuted form, the story of Emilia Viviani. In it also may be found a version of the story of Shelley's marriage with Harriet Westbrook, and his parting from her.[10]

This hint has proved so attractive to later Shelleyans that *Lodore* has become, to quote Sylva Norman, "a competition ground" for biographical interpretations.[11] Unfortunately, such an approach, while understandable in view of the novel's lack of intrinsic merit, obscures our perception of what Mary apparently was about both in *Lodore* and in the novel which follows it, *Falkner*.

Lodore, begun sometime around very early 1832[12] and evidently finished in the following year,[13] was not published until 1835, after a series of exasperating delays on the publisher's part.[14] The novel can be briefly described in terms of the destinies of seven of its characters, each of whom has a generally accepted biographical identification. Lord Lodore (aspects of Byron) returns to England as a jaded man in his mid-thirties and marries a beautiful girl of sixteen, Cornelia Santerre (either Harriet Westbrook or Annabella Milbanke). The marriage is not a success, largely because of the interference of Cornelia's mother, Lady Santerre, whose prototype may have been Eliza Westbrook, Judith Milbanke, or Mrs. Clermont, but who, in any case, is "a wordly woman and an oily flatterer."[15] After a year of marriage, Cornelia gives birth to a daughter, Ethel (either Augusta Ada Byron or Ianthe Elizabeth Shelley, in the beginning, and then becoming transformed into Mary herself). Not long after his marriage, Lord Lodore, because of complications arising from his dissolute past, is compelled to leave England, and he takes his infant daughter with him, while Lady Lodore returns to her mother.

Lodore, who leaves for America with Ethel, settles in a forest wilderness. There twelve years pass, and Ethel grows into a lovely girl of fifteen. But at this point, Lodore, fearing that his daughter's lack of experience with a social world may cause her grief in later years, decides to return with her to Europe. Unhappily for him, and for the aptness of Mary's title, he is killed in New York in a duel; and the novel is left to make its way along (with increasing triviality) for two more volumes without the presence of its titular hero. Fortunately, all turns out well: Ethel marries Edward Villiers (aspects of Shelley), passes with him through some annoying financial difficulties (clearly reminiscent of Mary's experiences with Shelley in late 1814), and wins through to a life of affluence and sentimentalized contentment.

Nor has Cornelia, Lodore's widow and Ethel's mother, been idle. Freed somewhat from the restrictions of an excessive artificiality by the death of her own mother, she engages in a flirtation with Horatio Saville (Shelley again, only more so); fails to realize the depth of his sincerity and of her own affection for him; and awakens one day to discover that Saville, while abroad, has married the daughter of a Neapolitan nobleman, Clorinda (Emilia Viviani). At this juncture in the novel, triviality gives way to unintentional farce, for Clorinda is so passionately jealous and possessive that she breaks a blood vessel during one of her fits of temper and then conveniently expires when Saville looks with admiration at a portrait in oils of a woman reputed to resemble Cornelia. Presumably a believer evermore in the hidden power of art, Saville returns to England, marries Cornelia (who becomes Viscountess Maristow); and the two pairs of lovers, we may assume, live happily ever after— or at least until the revolutions of 1848 reduce all of them to hysteria.

Such material defies almost any effort of the critical intelligence, and it is obvious why a biographical reading dominates the approach to *Lodore*. But it is possible, by the use of two or three external clues, to discover the probable "moral" intention that Mary had in mind (perhaps as a salve to her literary conscience) as she worked on *Lodore* and then on the novel which followed it, *Falkner*. First of all, we must realize that Mary held consciously to the belief that it was the responsibility of the novelist "to instruct and elevate, and not, as is too usual with writers of fiction, to amuse, and even corrupt."[16] Furthermore, in a letter to Charles Ollier of early 1833, she claimed that the true point of *Lodore* was that it demonstrated the "Vanity" of all "except the genuine affections of the heart."[17]

But while this latter point is, in a sense, the same "moral" as that found in *Valperga* and *Perkin Warbeck, Lodore* and its successor, *Falkner,* are markedly inferior to them as novels for at least one crucial reason: in the earlier books, the implied argument for the primacy of "the genuine affections of the heart" is presented against a background of concrete relevance—both Castruccio and Richard move in a world of political struggle. In *Lodore* and *Falkner,* however, the "moral" is tested against nothing more than a backdrop of theatrical vagueness. For, if we strip away all the biographical coincidences which clot Mary's last two novels, we discover that their eponymous heroes—Lord Lodore and Rupert John Falkner—are essentially composed of Mary's prosaic re-rendering of the gloomy protagonists that moved through Byron's earlier poetry.

And I suspect a critical remark of hers, written only two years after the publication of *Falkner,* reveals the moral intention that Mary mistakenly believed would inform her last two novels with significance. In a sharp attack upon what, for Mary, was the Byronic effect on character, she tells us: "Madame de Staël . . . is the founder of the Byronic school [and makes] the chief feeling of her work impatience of life under sorrow, suicide in despair. This at once blights existence. To feel that adversity and prosperity are both lessons to teach us a higher wisdom, the fruition of which we hope hereafter to inherit, and which at the same time is the ornament and crown of good men during life, ought to be the aim of every writer."[18] That is, Lord Lodore and Rupert John Falkner are characters who are deliberately drawn by Mary with the vices of "the Byronic school"—excessive pride, an ingrained misanthropy, a tendency to self-immolation in despair—and who are redeemed in the course of their presentation (Lodore less fully than Falkner) by the transforming power of "the genuine affections of the heart."

Yet the curious inexactness of the title to *Lodore* indicates that Mary failed to control fully the theme she had originally planned.[19] Indeed, one of the most enfeebling things about her fifth novel is the air of desperate improvisation it frequently suggests after the death of Lodore in New York. Consequently, it seems reasonable to regard *Falkner* as a more skillful treatment on Mary's part of an intention she was unable to handle adequately in the novel which preceded it.

Written apparently as a direct result of the commercial success of *Lodore,*[20] *Falkner* holds the reader's attention a good deal more consistently than does the other novel. It opens with two chapters of background information concerning a six-year-old orphaned girl, Elizabeth Raby, about whose origins and connections there is some mystery. Then, in the third chapter, we are introduced to Falkner, a man who, to quote from Mary's criticism of "the Byronic school," surely is possessed by "impatience of life under sorrow, suicide in despair." For Falkner has come to the quiet village where Elizabeth lives to commit suicide. Fortunately for him, and for the aptness of Mary's title, as Falkner pulls the trigger to kill himself, Elizabeth seizes his arm and makes the ball whiz "harmlessly by his ear."[21] The consequence of this interference is that, within a few days, the melancholy Falkner and the orphaned child are together on their way to London, and they proceed from there on a long period of wandering across Europe and Russia.

The remainder of the novel deals with what are essentially four lines of related development: the growing tenderness between Falkner and Elizabeth, and the effect this has upon his character; the gradual uncovering of his guilty past (through his self-will he has been the unintentional cause of a virtuous woman's drowning); Falkner's eventual reconcilement with himself and with society; and the uncovering of Elizabeth's own antecedents and her attainment of marital happiness with Gerard Neville, the son of the woman unintentionally destroyed by Falkner. With these four plot lines completed, the novel ends with what is perhaps a revelation of Mary's psychological needs as a woman: although Elizabeth is, of course, blissfully married to Gerard Neville, Falkner continues to live nearby; and he is an ever-present source of paternal comfort and of undemanding nonsexual love.

Falkner, then, although not an important novel, easily surpasses *Lodore* in readability and coherence. Moreover, even this brief inspection of it reveals, I think, that a minor critical problem raised by the character of Falkner himself can be readily resolved. Briefly, that problem resides in the question of whether Falkner's character owes more to Trelawny or to Byron. (At such a level of commentary does the criticism of Mary's last novels move.) Elizabeth Nitchie, for example, has shown with scholarly thoroughness that a good many of the surface details that shape Rupert John Falkner were drawn from Mary's personal knowledge of Edward John Trelawny and from Trelawny's "autobiography," *The Adventures of a Younger Son* (1831).[22] She therefore concludes: "Falkner owes more to . . . Trelawny than to Byron."[23]

But Trelawny was himself something of a by-product of Byron's earlier poetry. Indeed, even Byron considered Trelawny's manner as such an absurd attempt to carry out the leading characteristics of the "Corsair" that the poet ruefully commented to Teresa Guiccioli on the eeriness of the resemblance.[24] Furthermore, as we now know, *The Adventures of a Younger Son* is in no real sense an autobiography; it is a projection of Trelawny's romanticized fantasies of himself.[25] As a result, it seems evident enough that no actual conflict exists between the possible influences of Byron and Trelawny on the characterization of Falkner. Much of what Mary took from Trelawny was already imbued with elements of "the Byronic school." And the character of Falkner, as it exists in the novel, is obviously Mary's moralistic patchwork of Byronic egoism, subsequent (inevitable) despair, and final regeneration through the power of love. Unhappily, the complete irrelevance of Mary's concern with Byronism is revealed most clearly by the changed taste evident in the reading public of 1837: for by then, when she published *Falkner* with its exhausted vein of Byronic echoes, Victoria had come to the throne; and Dickens' first novel—with its benevolently muddle-headed protagonist, Samuel Pickwick— had appeared in volume form to delight still further a reading public far different from the one that had, more than twenty years earlier, bought ten thousand copies of Byron's *Corsair* in a single day.

II *Shorter Fiction*

The bulk of Mary's shorter fiction belongs to the period after Shelley's death, and the general strictures which have been made about her last three novels (and especially her last two)—their paucity of serious ideas, their excessive sentimentality, their lack of creative vigor—can be applied even more severely to her work in the shorter forms. As Mary herself realized, she required, even at her best, a good deal of space;[26] and the want of it merely intensified her weaknesses. "Vast events," to cite Muriel Spark, "general ideas, passions like ambition and universal love, are what Mary manipulates with ease."[27] But these subjects, we might add, are essentially novelistic ones. As a result, the absence of emotional and intellectual significance that we have noted in Mary's fiction as the years passed after Shelley's death is nowhere seen more nakedly than in her short stories.

Yet a partial exception is *Mathilda,* and it is interesting to note that this work was written while Shelley was still alive and that in length—it runs to over seventy-five pages of text in its modern edition—it is not really a short story at all.

Unpublished during Mary's lifetime, *Mathilda* was composed between August 4 and September 12, 1819, and revised slightly in early November, shortly before the birth of Percy Florence.[28]

Briefly, the narrative concerns three characters—Mathilda herself, who although now near death, is the narrator; Mathilda's father, a widower, who more than two years earlier, had revealed his incestuous desire for her and had then fled in self-horror to die (an apparent suicide) by drowning during a storm; and Woodville, a brilliant young poet, who has become friendly with Mathilda after her father's death, but whose kindness to her has been repaid with captiousness and irritability. The *novella* ends with Mathilda poised on the brink of death (her final illness is precipitated by a night outdoors in inclement weather) and with her thoughts centered on two reflections: remorse for her cruel responses to Woodville's kindnesses, and anticipation at the imminent "eternal mental union" with her father's spirit.

Naturally enough, such material, written as it was in the summer and autumn of 1819, has invited its share of biographical interpretation. Although biographical interpretations—with their inevitable tendency to oversimplify—are perhaps the most treacherous of critical approaches, some degree of certainty in interpretation seems possible. For one thing, Mathilda's remorse over her treatment of the kindhearted Woodville appears to have a concrete analogue in Mary's own awareness of her self-centered anguish in 1818–19 over the death of her two children, Clara and William, and of her apparent rejection of Shelley's sympathy. For another, as we cannot help knowing, Godwin, in marked contrast to Shelley, failed Mary lamentably in her time of need. During the period of her deepest grief, in fact, her father's letters, almost totally devoid of human sympathy, reflect, for the most part, a rather chilling absorption in his own financial difficulties.[29] We can therefore infer as reasonable this biographical reading: that an evident psychological aspect of *Mathilda* is its presentation of a beloved father figure who becomes morally repulsive in his daughter's eyes and who literally "dies" to her. That is, *Mathilda* seems to represent something of Mary's resentment over her father's failure to respond to her emotional needs, and it perhaps suggests also an unconscious pattern of revenge upon him.

Woodville, on the other hand, seemingly reflects Mary's awareness of her culpability in rejecting Shelley's proffered kindness. Thus Mathilda's harsh treatment of Woodville apparently offers some confirmation of the widely accepted theory that in 1818–19 a serious breach developed in the Shelley marriage because of Mary's anguish over the loss of her children.[30] Indeed, it is possible to find in *Mathilda* evidence of something perhaps even more significant. For it is clearly one thing to write, as Shelley has done in *The Cenci,* a study of incest that reveals, in its dramatic form, an objective structure with symbolic implications about the nature of political and moral tyranny. It is something else to write, as Mary has, a first-person narrative in which the central and climactic moment turns upon the irrational and repulsive nature of sexual desire itself. Interestingly enough, Godwin thought the subject of *Mathilda* "disgusting and detestable,"[31] a verdict which surely had much to do with the work's remaining unpublished during Mary's lifetime.

In short, I suggest that *Mathilda* sheds a good deal of light on Shelley's complaint in "Epipsychidion" that he has been condemned to lie "within a chaste cold bed" (l. 299). Quite plausibly, Mary, already having lost three children, was no longer able to look upon sexuality as the ultimate source of happiness or of fulfillment. Rather, as *Mathilda* implies through the drowning of the heroine's father and through Mathilda's own subsequent wasting away in unhealthy isolation, sexual desire has become, within the context of the *novella,* merely a prelude to death. And the consequences of such a state of mind, if my reading is correct, apparently has only one outcome: confronted by Shelley's physical desire, Mary might well have retreated into frigidity. "The cold chaste Moon" of "Epipsychidion," in other words, expresses her own pathos as well as Shelley's.

But, aside from this biographical interpretation, *Mathilda* is also susceptible to a reading which places it, like *Frankenstein,* in an interesting relationship to Shelley's *Alastor.* For the *novella,* like the poem, is concerned primarily with one of the most prevalent themes in English literature since the rise of the novel in the eighteenth century—the exploration of the conflict between the individual sensibility and the demands upon it implicit within the context of social existence. Thus both *Mathilda* and *Alastor* present their material in the form of what, in essence, is a triangle. On the one hand, Mathilda is depicted as being torn between the anguished recollection of her father's impossible love for her (impossible, that is, in terms of what is beyond the individual sensibility: society and its code of morality) and the much lower intensity of Woodville's socially regulated and eminently rational friendship.[32] On the other hand, the unnamed poet in *Alastor* is presented as intent on the attainment of an equally impossible love—"a veiled maid" whose voice is "like the voice of his soul" (ll. 151–53). And his vulnerability to this hopeless dream of possessing an objectified self (an interesting variation on the theme of incest) has been prepared for by his refusal to acknowledge the reality of any love beyond the limits of his own sensibility—hence his absolute indifference to the "real"—the socially demonstrable—love proffered him by the "Arab maiden" in the poem (ll. 129–40).

Mathilda, then, like *Alastor,* contains a suggestive exploration of a much-handled theme. Moreover, the fact that Mary's subject evolves from incestuous desire gives to her treatment an interest which is independent of the poem. For, of all social taboos, that against the commission of incest is perhaps the strongest; and to present, as Mary does in *Mathilda,* a central figure who is destroyed by the consequences of incestuous desire—a central figure, moreover, who anticipates achieving by her death an "eternal mental union" with her guilty father—is to underscore strikingly the apparently unbridgeable gap between the individual sensibility and the social world outside it. ("Incest is," as Shelley remarked less than a week after Mary had finished *Mathilda,* "a very poetical circumstance."[33]) In short, although *Mathilda* resembles *Alastor* in many respects (including the nearly identical wanderings of Mathilda's father and the unnamed poet), the theme of incest crudely and sharply focuses on an element which is frequently concealed in Shelley's much-debated poem: the final defense of the psyche against the encroachment of a social world is a flight into death. (Perhaps, significantly, Mathilda's death grows directly out of Woodville's absence; and Woodville's absence is due to that most archetypal of social ties: he is away on a visit to his mother.)

In summary, the theme of incest functions in *Mathilda* as a pervasive metaphor. Starkly, it represents that which society, with its moral code, most abhors. Indeed, both Mathilda and her father, as social beings, abhor the idea of incest themselves. But, when the *novella* ends, Mathilda, as we have seen, is poised on the brink of an eternal union with her father—very much as the nameless poet's death at the end of *Alastor* preserves (and, indeed, enlarges) the integrity of his dream. That is, by suggesting that death represents the triumph of the individual sensibility over social "reality," *Mathilda* can be regarded as shedding light not only backward upon *Alastor* but forward upon *Adonais*—and perhaps even upon Shelley's most problematic poem, *The Triumph of Life.*

Aside from Mathilda and a handful of stories like "A Tale of the Passions" (set in thirteenth-century Italy), "The Bride of Modern Italy" (an early attempt to make fictional material from the Emilia Viviani episode in Shelley's life), and "The Heir of Mondolfo" (a feeble tale of true love triumphing over a father's tyrannical opposition to having a lowborn woman for a daughter-in-law), the overwhelming bulk of Mary's short stories—at least seventeen in number—were published in the years 1829–39.[34] Unhappily, however, none of Mary's ventures in the short story, either early or late, possesses much intrinsic interest for the modern reader.

Occasionally, it is true, a successful effect is achieved—as, for example, in "Ferdinando Eboli" in which Mary is able to arouse genuine suspense through her manipulation of her concept of the double (the hero discovers that his happy and prominent role in life has been appropriated in his absence by a man who looks exactly like him). But the interest is quickly dissipated by a clumsy, natural explanation: the double is simply Ferdinando's older, illegitimate brother who resents his own shabby position in life. Again, in "Transformation" Mary returns to the concept of the double; but this time she treats the subject more in the manner of a fairy tale (the hero is tricked by a dwarf with supernatural powers into exchanging bodies and then discovers, almost too late, that the dwarf has no intention of ever restoring his original shape). But, although "Ferdinando Eboli" and "Transformation" are both above the average for Mary's stories, we have only to think of Poe's "William Wilson" (not to mention Dostoevski's "The Double") to realize that she has done very little to explore the potential richness of her subject.

However, the kind of audience Mary was writing for presents a partial explanation of this general lack of substance. Fully fifteen of her stories were first published in the *Keepsake,* one of the many annuals which flourished in the England of the 1820's and 1830's. But, if we turn to George Eliot's remarkably accurate re-creation of that period, we find this assessment of Mary's major market (in *Middlemarch,* Book III, Chapter 27):

Mr. Ned Plymbale . . . was in *tête-à-tête* with Rosamund. He had brought the last *Keepsake,* the gorgeous watered-silk publication which marked modern progress at that time; and he considered himself very fortunate that he could be the first to look over it with her, dwelling on the ladies and gentlemen with shiny copper-plate cheeks and copper-plate smiles, and pointing to comic verses as capital and sentimental stories as interesting. . . .

Mr. Ned smiled nervously, while Lydgate drawing the *Keepsake* towards him and opening it, gave a short scornful laugh and tossed up his chin, as if in wonderment at human folly. . . .

"I wonder which would turn out to be the silliest—the engravings or the writing here," said Lydgate. . . . "Do look at this bridegroom coming out of church: did you ever see such a 'sugared invention?' . . . Yet I will answer for it the story makes him one of the first gentlemen in the land."

With few exceptions, the contributors to these collections must have been aware of the quality of writing expected from them— and Mary, it must be conceded, rarely rose above the level of the expectation.

Mention might be made, of course, about the intermittent flashes of humor in "The Moral Immortal" (first published in the *Keepsake* for 1834); for Mary is rarely credited with a sense of fun in her fiction. In this story—an apparent parody of her father's *St. Leon*—the narration begins with this announcement: "July 16, 1833.—This is a memorable anniversary for me; on it I complete my three hundred and twenty-third year!"[35] The narrator then proceeds—and his name, "Winzy," should alert us to the fact that Mary is keeping her tongue in cheek—to give an account of his early history. A pupil of Cornelius Agrippa, Winzy one day drinks the elixir of immortality, mistakenly thinking it is a potion to cure him of his love for Bertha. Afterward, informed of the true nature of the potion given him by Agrippa, Winzy marries Bertha and passes some years in happiness before the discrepancy between his own ever-youthful appearance and her necessarily aging one becomes evident.

"At length," Winzy tells us, "she insinuated that I must share my secret with her, and bestow on her like benefits to those I myself enjoyed, or she would denounce me—and then she burst into tears." But since Winzy, of course, does not possess the secret of mixing a new draught of the elixir, Bertha's resentment understandably increases: "On one occasion, fancying that the belle of the village regarded me with favouring eyes, she brought me a gray wig. Her constant discourse among her acquaintances was, that though I looked so young, there was ruin at work within my frame; and she affirmed that the worst symptom about me was my apparent health."

Despite this occasional (and unexpected) lightness of touch,

"The Mortal Immortal," like Mary's other short stories, fails to develop into anything significant. Bertha eventually dies; Winzy lives on and on; and the story ends with his determination, like the Walton at the opening of *Frankenstein,* to search out "the powers of frost in their home." If he returns, he will be a benefactor to mankind; if not, he will have "set at liberty the life imprisoned within" his mortal frame. With such an incongruous ending before us, we can conclude that Mary, aside from any question of the kind of market she had, was hopelessly handicapped within a brief number of pages. Quite clearly, she needed much more space than the short story provided to develop adequately the themes and subjects which were most congenial to her talent; and her unhappy solution, as Bradford Booth has indicated, was to attempt "to force the plot for a complete novel into a dozen or a score of pages."[36]

III *Verse*

Mary's longest poetic efforts are the two blank-verse dramas she wrote in 1820, *Proserpine* and *Midas,* both of which are essentially close adaptations of the corresponding tales in Ovid's *Metamorphoses.* In the first, and superior effort, *Proserpine,* Mary succeeds in presenting, gracefully and economically, the well-known story of the abduction and qualified return of Ceres' daughter. Unfortunately, the presence of two of Shelley's lyrics in the drama— Ino's song, "Arethusa arose/From her couch of snows"; and Proserpine's "Sacred Goddess, Mother Earth"—reveals unmistakably that the pleasant lines on either side of them belong to a competent versifier rather than to a poet. For, although neither song deserves to be placed among Shelley's best, both of them demonstrate, by the heightened quality of their effect upon the reader, what has been missing from Mary's own verses: poetry itself. And if this is true for *Proserpine,* it is even truer for *Midas,* where, embedded among lines somewhat less skillfully handled than those in *Proserpine,* we again find two of Shelley's own poems: Apollo's song, "The sleepless Hours who watch me as I lie"; and Pan's, "From the forests and highlands/We come, we come." In short, the blank verse of Mary's two poetic dramas belongs to a sensitive, intelligent prose writer with a fairly good ear.[37]

But, aside from *Proserpine* and *Midas,* Mary also wrote a number of shorter poems, the most interesting of which are two: "The

Choice," composed soon after Shelley's death; and "A Dirge,"
published for the first time in the *Keepsake* of 1831, and then again,
in revised form, as part of the notes to her edition of Shelley's poetry
in 1839.[38] Since "The Choice" has already been briefly discussed
in connection with Mary's early reaction to Shelley's death (see
Chapter 4, Section I), little more need be said about it. Written
in heroic couplets and running to over 150 lines, Mary's poem of
retrospection and self-recrimination confirms, rather unflatteringly,
her confession to Maria Gisborne in 1835: "I can never write
verses except under the influence of a strong sentiment and seldom
even then."[39]

For "The Choice," although generally superior to *Proserpine*
and *Midas* in the effectiveness of its versification, achieves only
intermittently, in its meandering presentation of Mary's reflections,
the condition of genuine poetry. As a result, for every occasional
stroke of memorable imagery or thought—"As fireflies gleam
through interlunar nights"; "Whose flowers now star the dark
earth near his tomb"; "The wife of Time no more, I wed Eternity"—
we are repaid with dreary stretches that remind us, all too embar-
rassingly for Mary's sake, of Shelley's own poetry:

> *Infant immortal!* [i.e., *William*] *chosen for the sky!*
> *No grief upon thy brow's young purity*
> *Entrenched sad lines, or blotted with its might*
> *The sunshine of thy smile's celestial light;—*
> *The image shattered, the bright spirit fled,*
> *Thou shin'st the evening star among the dead.*[40]

Altogether, then, "The Choice" is a poem which, had it not been
written by the wife of Shelley, would have little real claim on our
attention today.

Nor is "A Dirge" entirely exempt from the same criticism. Indeed,
as Frederick L. Jones has pointed out, almost all of Mary's shorter
poems originate from an identical impulse—her grief over the loss
of Shelley.[41] Thus in "A Dirge," a poem Mary herself considered
"the best . . . I ever wrote,"[42] we hear the old familiar notes of
grief and irremediable loss and distracting self-pity being rung in
again:

> *This morn they gallant bark, Love*
> *Sailed on a sunny sea;*

Tis noon, and tempests dark, Love,
 Have wrecked it on the lee.

Ah Woe—ah woe—ah woe
 By spirits of the deep,
He's cradled on the billow,
 To his unwaking sleep!

Thou liest upon the shore, Love
 Beside the knelling surge,
But sea-nymphs ever more, Love,
 Shall sadly chaunt thy dirge.

O come, O come—O come!
 Ye spirits of the deep!
While near his sea-weed pillow,
 My lonely watch I keep.

From far across the sea, Love,
 I hear a wild lament,
By Echo's voice from thee, Love,
 From Ocean's cavern sent:

O list! O list! O list!
 The spirits of the deep—
Loud sounds their wail of sorrow—
 While I for ever weep![43]

For, while this poem is not unpleasant in its musical quality, it does suggest that Mary's deepest sympathies actually lay with Shelley's "secondary style" (the phrase is Procter's, and it was used to describe Mary's own poetry[44]). That is—and this is a point that is recurred to in the discussion of Mary's notes to Shelley's poetry (in the following chapter in section III)—Mary, if we may judge from her single most successful poem after Shelley's death, responded most naturally and enthusiastically to the lesser Shelley: to the Shelley who had a fondness for creating a passive self-image in order to lavish pity upon it, and to the Shelley whom adverse critics (for example, Matthew Arnold and F. R. Leavis) have found so easy to erect as a strawman for contemptuous dismissal.

CHAPTER 6

Nonfictional Prose

THERE can be little doubt that Mary's best writing, after she had finished *The Last Man,* went into her nonfictional prose of the 1830's and 1840's. For, although it is true that the fiction subsequent to her third novel possesses its own kind of interest as a potentially illuminating (and certainly distressing) anticlimax to a most promising novelistic beginning, the nonfictional prose reassures us, by its intrinsic content, of the genuine strength of Mary Shelley's mind. Emotionally confused, psychologically isolated, financially troubled, Mary yet managed to drive her pen across more than two thousand pages of nonfictional prose in less than a decade—pages which reveal her to be, in the totality of their impression, perhaps the one female novelist in England before George Eliot with a breadth of intellectual interests that might be called European rather than English. In this chapter, then, three specific areas of her nonfiction are considered in an ascending order of importance: (1) her *Rambles in Germany and Italy* (1844); (2) her biographical writings, with specific emphasis placed upon the five volumes of *Lives* she wrote for Lardner's *Cabinet Cyclopedia* (1835–39); and (3) her editing and annotation of Shelley's poetry and prose ([1824,] 1839–40).

I *Rambles in Germany and Italy*

If, of the works of Mary's early career, *Valperga* is the one which seems to be most associated with misfortune, then surely, of her later career, *Rambles in Germany and Italy,* her last published work, deserves the same doubtful distinction. Begun with apparent confidence and high spirits,[1] continued in illness with only a dogged desire for money to keep her pen moving;[2] the *Rambles* was published by Moxon in two volumes in July, 1844. But, although the reviewers were polite and sometimes flattering,[3] and although modern criticism of it has (with one exception) agreed to rank the *Rambles* as "one of the best things Mary ever wrote,"[4] the fact that

Mary's account of her continental travels in 1840, and 1842–43 has never been reprinted indicates clearly enough its qualified success.

Moreover, the indirect aftermath of the book's publication involved Mary in perhaps the most painful emotional disappointment she suffered in the years after Shelley's death.[5] For the motive which drove her pen so diligently through illness and low spirits—her desire to make money from the *Rambles*—was in no ordinary sense a selfish one: she wanted the money to help pay the debts of a young man she had first met in Paris in the summer of 1843, a political exile from Italy named Gatteschi. Unhappily for her, Gatteschi repaid her kindness (and her effusive fondness for him in her letters) by trying to blackmail her in the latter half of 1845, one year after the *Rambles* had been published.[6] Driven nearly to distraction by the attempt, made painfully conscious that she was, after all, only a middle-aged woman whose romantic days had ended, Mary wrote to Claire on September 15, 1845, in an agony of self-disgust: "I will only write a few words—for I am too agitated—I am indeed humbled—& feel all my vanity & folly & pride—my credulity I can forgive in myself but not my want of common sense—& worse—my self reproaches are indeed keen."[7]

And yet, as if to restore Mary's faith in the motto with which her journal truly ends—"Preserve always a habit of giving,"[8] another young man she had befriended, Alexander Andrew Knox, came forward and successfully countermined Gatteschi. Knox, who went to Paris with the specific intention of regaining Mary's letters, achieved his objective with a liberal bribe; had all of Gatteschi's papers seized and brought to the office of M. Delessert, the prefect of the Parisian police; extracted from them Mary's correspondence; and returned her "stupid nonsensical letters"[9] to her soon afterward, undoubtedly for destruction. It was, altogether, a hectic (and pathetic) conclusion to Mary's career as a "society widow."

The *Rambles,* presented in the form of letters, is divided into two unequal parts. Part I, by far the shorter, runs to approximately half of the first section, or volume, and covers the period from June 13, 1840, to October 12, 1840; it describes Mary's itinerary from England (with her son Percy) to Paris (where they were joined by two of Percy's college friends), to Cadenabbia on Lake Como (for almost a two-month stay), to Milan (where the misplacement of a letter caused Mary an unexpected delay), and then back to

Paris again by way of Geneva. Part II, which covers the period from June, 1842, to July 10, 1843, relates how Mary, along with Percy and Alexander Andrew Knox, passed extended stays at Kissingen (where Mary undertook the *Kur* at the mineral baths), at Dresden (where the well-known composer, Henry Hugh Pearson, joined their party for a time), at Venice (where Mary was painfully reminded of the death of Clara Everina more than twenty years earlier), at Rome (where Mary spent a good deal of time looking at works of art), and then at Sorrento (where, after a brief excursion to Amalfi, Mary's account of her travels ends). More specifically, three aspects of the *Rambles* seem worth brief attention: Mary's use of reminiscence; the question of Gatteschi's contributions to the work; and the noticeably uneven quality of the writing. As for Mary's use of reminiscence, it is easy enough to see how references to the past provided her with a means of emotionally heightening her material. Thus, when entering an inn in Italy for the first time in many years, she describes her reactions in this fashion: "Window-curtains, the very wash-hand stands, they were all such as had been familiar to me in Italy long, long ago. I had not seen them since those young and happy days. Strange and indescribable emotions invaded me; recollections, long forgotten, arose fresh and strong by mere force of association, produced by those objects being presented to my eye, inspiring a mixture of pleasure and pain, almost amounting to agony" (I, 60–61).

Again, after sailing to Geneva on October 4, 1840, Mary presents the reader with her own sharp sense of loss as she recalls her stay on the shores of that same lake, almost a quarter of a century before, when she had been an eighteen-year-old girl, beginning the composition of *Frankenstein:*

It was not a pleasant day for my voyage. . . . The far Alps were hid; the wide lake looked drear. At length, I caught a glimpse of the scenes among which I had lived, when first I stepped out from childhood into life. There, on the shores of Bellerive, stood Diodati; and our humble dwelling, Maison Chapuis [*sic*], nestled close to the lake below. There were the terraces, the vineyards, the upward path threading them, the little port where our boat lay moored; I could mark and recognize a thousand slight peculiarities, familiar objects then—forgotten since—now replete with recollections and associations. Was I the same person who had lived there, the companion of the dead? For all were gone: even my young child [William], whom I had looked upon as the joy of future years. (I, 139–40)

Clearly, then, Mary's belief that her readers would be able to understand the references to her own past and to Shelley's—a belief not always well founded[10]—led her into a more than occasional reliance upon nostalgia and upon autobiographic allusion.[11]

A second aspect of the *Rambles* worth brief attention is the question of Gatteschi's contributions. For, although Gatteschi was to prove himself a contemptible person by his blackmail attempt, he undoubtedly did help Mary with the second volume of her travels. Writing to Claire Clairmont on July 1, 1844, Mary told her that Gatteschi had "furnished me daily with materials for my book";[12] and, soon afterward, when the publication of the *Rambles* was imminent, Mary declared that "the best parts" were Gatteschi's.[13] Such statements of indebtedness, however, probably need to be qualified by our awareness of Mary's emotional attitude toward Gatteschi at the time she wrote them. No doubt she was more than ready to exaggerate the value of his assistance, exactly as she was exaggerating his (apparently nonexistent) moral qualities; for she confessed to Claire after the blackmail attempt that she had regarded him for a long while as "an angel."[14] Perhaps it would be just, then, based on our limited knowledge of Gatteschi as a political exile from Italy, to credit him most surely with the background material to the two specifically political "chapters" in Volume II: Letter XIV (dealing with the history of the secret republican association known as the Carbonari) and Letter XXI (dealing with the insurrection of Romagna in 1831 and the occupation of Ancona by the French in early 1832).[15]

Doubtless, too, Gatteschi was responsible, at least indirectly, for Mary's rather prominent insistence on the need for Italian unification and independence. In her preface, she remarks, apropos of the "enthusiasm for liberty" in Italy, that "the country . . . is struggling with its fetters,—not only the material ones that weigh on it so heavily . . . but with those that have entered into and bind the soul—superstition, luxury, servility, indolence, violence, vice" (I, x). Later, during her account of her stay at Cadenabbia, she asserts her faith unequivocally in the success of what she believed Gatteschi was struggling for; but we cannot help noting as well that the unintended irony in the assertion redounded upon Mary within a year of publication:

I love the Italians. It is impossible to live among them and not love them. Their faults are many—the faults of the oppressed—love of pleasure, disregard of truth, indolence, and violence of temper. But their falsehood is on the surface—it is not deceit. Under free institutions, and where the acquirement of knowledge is not as now a mark inviting oppression and wrong, their love of pleasure were ennobled into intellectual activity. ... They are a noble race of men—a beautiful race of women; the time must come when again they will take a high place among nations. Their habits, fostered by their governments, alone are degraded and degrading. (I, 87)

But, despite these ascriptions of direct and indirect influence to Gatteschi, there can be little doubt, I think, that the *Rambles* is essentially Mary's. Whatever material Gatteschi gave her, Mary was still faced with the necessity of recasting it into narrative form; and anyone who reads even the two chapters that I have ascribed to Gatteschi finds in them Mary's own personal tone.

Last of all, there is the matter of the unevenness of Mary's style in the *Rambles*. At times she writes an excellent prose, as, for example, in this brief description of the "scirocco":

Nothing can be stranger than this scirocco: at its first breath the sea grows dull, leaden, slate-coloured—all its transparency is gone. The view of the opposite shore is hidden in mist. The near mountains wear a deeper green, but have lost all brightness and cast weird shadows on the dull waters. This wind coming from the south-east is with us a land wind. It rolls huge waves on the beach of Naples; but beneath our cliffs the sea is calm—such a calm!—it looks so treacherous, that even if you did not hear of the true state of things, you would hesitate to trust yourself to it. (II, 277–78)

Again, on occasion, she is well able to justify her promise to Moxon that she will make the *Rambles* as "amusing" as she can,[16] as in this account of her experiences at Milan with a group of American tourists who shared a table with her:

Sometimes I amuse myself by classifying the party. There is a round, good-humoured clergyman, with his family, who is the Curious Traveller. He is very earnest in search of knowledge, but gentlemanly and unintrusive. There is the Knowing Traveller: he pounced upon a poor little man sitting next to him, to-day. "So you have shopping,—making purchases; been horridly cheated, I'm sure. Those Italians are such rogues! What did you buy? What did you give for those gloves? Four *swanzigers*—you have been done! A *swanziger* and a-half—that's the price anywhere. Two *swanzigers* for the best gloves to be found in Milan—and those are not the best."

This gratuitous piece of misinformation made the poor purchaser blush up
to the eyes with shame at his own folly. (I, 120)

But passages like this one must be balanced against tiresome
stretches of quite feeble art criticism. "There is another picture,"
Mary tells us in her account of the art of early Florence, "which
to see, is to feel the happiness which the soul receives from objects
presented to the eye, that kindle and elevate the imagination. It
represents the Adoration of the Magi. . . . There is one of the
Kings standing on one side of the Virgin, which might . . . create a
passion in a woman's heart. Where on earth find a man so full of
majesty, gentleness, and feeling?" (II, 143). This tone of strained
and unconvincing enthusiasm, liberally sprinkled with clichés,
reaches its nadir of hollow-sounding praise in Letter XVIII with
Mary's approach to the *Apollo Belvedere:* "As I entered the com-
partment in which he stands, a divine presence seemed to fill the
chamber." (Perhaps the best way of grasping the deficiency of
Mary's writing about art is to read Chapter 4 of Samuel Butler's
The Way of All Flesh with its incisive deflation of the English traveler's insistence on having the properly "sublime" reactions during
his tour.)

Too, there is at times a disconcerting habit on Mary's part of
evading the task of description by resorting to that most time-
worn (and shabbiest) of rhetorical excuses—the inadequacy of
words. Thus, after leaving Trarbach on the Moselle, Mary tells
us that she passed through "the finest scenery." "But words are
vain," she continues, "and in description there must ever be at
once a vagueness and a sameness that conveys no distinct ideas,
unless it should awaken the imagination" (I, 23). And she resorts
to the same rusty device thirty pages later: "What words can
express—for indeed, for many ideas and emotions there are no
words—the feelings excited by the tumult, the uproar and matchless
beauty of a cataract, with its eternal, ever-changing veil of misty
spray?" (I, 51).

But even in this just-quoted instance she has not exhausted her
variations on the theme of the inadequacy of words—one that
was hardly worth playing the first time; for, when she arrives at
Lake Como she remarks: "Descriptions with difficulty convey
definite impressions, and any picture or print of our part of the lake
will better than my words describe the scenery around us" (I, 66).

It is no wonder that Browning, when he came to read the *Rambles,* commented sharply on Mary's penchant for "looking wisely up at the sun, clouds, evening star, or mountain top and wisely saying 'who shall describe *that* sight!' "[17] Altogether, then, the *Rambles* is a work of uneven quality. Often quite interesting and undoubtedly superior to all of the fiction published after *Perkin Warbeck,* the *Rambles* contains, even today, a good deal of pleasure for the reader. At the same time, it must face the charge—and accept the verdict—of failing to display the consistent originality of impression that is to be found in the best travel literature.

II *Mary Shelley and Biography*

Although a recent article on Mary Shelley—"Mary Shelley, Traveler"—has argued persuasively for seeing her sustained interest in travel as an important key to her personality and achievement,[18] an equally sound argument might be made for the significance of her extensive interest in biography. (For that matter, *Perkin Warbeck* itself—as well as *Valperga*—has its genuine foundation in biography.) As early as 1814, when she was only seventeen years of age, she had begun a life of Jean Baptiste Louvet, the minor French journalist and politician.[19] In the early 1820's she wrote at least two articles of a biographical nature—"Madame D'Houtetot" (published in the third number of *The Liberal*)[20] and the now lost reminiscence of Lord Byron:[21] and she also composed the eleven pages of fragmentary notes on the life of Shelley which Thomas Jefferson Hogg used many years later.[22] In the latter half of the 1820's she gave Thomas Moore significant assistance with his biography of Byron, evidently writing out her recollections for his use[23]—very much as, a year or two later, she provided Cyrus Redding with "nearly all the matter" which he used for his brief sketch of Shelley in the Galignani edition of the poetry (1829).[24]

Furthermore, during this same period, Mary countered John Murray's refusal to publish *Perkin Warbeck* with an offer, on November 12, 1829, to write for him the lives of Madame de Staël and Empress Josephine.[25] And, although there was to be no immediate outcome to Mary's proposal to Murray, it is probably in this early mention of Madame de Staël that we find the true origin of her most extended venture into biographical writing—the five volumes of *Lives* she published in Lardner's *Cabinet Cyclopedia*

in the years 1835–39—a series which, ranging across four nations
and six centuries, concluded with a fifty-page survey of the life and
work of Madame de Staël.[26]

Nor does this rather extensive enumeration exhaust the list of
Mary's biographical interests. Aside from other proposals to
Murray in 1829–30 to write "a life of Mahomet," or "The Lives
of the English Philosophers," or the "Lives of Celebrated Wom-
en,"[27] Mary also planned to write a biography of her father; and
she went so far as to compose a series of notes for the task in 1836–
37.[28] Indeed, the writing of Mary's which many critics consider
the most important that she ever did—her prefaces and notes to
Shelley's poetry and prose (see below, Section III)—can scarcely be
regarded as other than essentially biographical.

But as we give specific attention to biography, the larger question
arises of whether Mary's sustained interest indicates anything of
a more general significance for an understanding of her career.
Conservatively, of course, it is easy enough to dismiss the question
by referring to two obvious facts: Mary's need for earning money
with her pen and her experiences with noteworthy people combined
to lead her inevitably into a good deal of biographical writing. But,
despite the justice of these observations, something more significant
does seem possible. For, although the central literary impulse of
the age was toward the projection of the self in one form or another
of simulated autobiography (Byron's *Childe Harold,* Wordsworth's
The Prelude, Hazlitt's *Liber Amoris,* Coleridge's *Biographia Liter-
aria,* the innumerable lyrics from major and minor poets), Mary
Shelley often exhibited a sense of restraint about self-revelation
(as, for example, the bulk of her journal entries indicate) that seems
to provide another instance of her constitutional link with the
eighteenth century.

Consequently, the literary usage to which she puts her own personality and experiences, pronounced as it may seem in her fiction
(and even, occasionally, in her nonfiction), is balanced by the literary attention she gives to the lives of others outside her own immediate experience. Thus, in her sketch of Metastasio in the Italian
Lives, she makes the following comment on the usefulness of certain
extracts she has quoted from his letters: "It is from passages such
as these . . . that we can collect the peculiar character of the man—
his difference from others—and the mechanism of being that
rendered him the individual that he was. Such, Dr. Johnson remarks,

is the true end of biography, and he recommends the bringing forward of minute, yet characteristic details, as essential to this style of history; to follow which precept has been the aim and desire of the writer of these pages" (II, 206).

The value of this comment is twofold. First, it reveals how the impulse of the age toward psychological exploration could be directed outward, toward the psychology of others (no doubt the increasing importance of the novel as a literary form in the nineteenth century has a basis here). Second, and more specifically, the citation of Dr. Johnson as the approved model for biographers suggests a concept of literary "decorum" somewhat surprising in view of Mary's fiction. Furthermore, the approving reference to Dr. Johnson is hardly accidental. In February, 1835, shortly after the first volume of her *Lives* for Lardner's *Cabinet Cyclopedia* had appeared, Mary wrote to John Murray to tell him how fond she was of "the kind-hearted wise & gentle Bear" who, she thought, was "as loveable a friend as a profound philosopher."[29]

Two years later, when Mary published her third volume in the *Cabinet Cyclopedia* (the *Lives* dealing with Spanish and Portuguese writers), Mary included a passage on Cervantes' failure to write an autobiography which sounds rather like a variation on *Rasselas* or "The Vanity of Human Wishes," as well as implicitly revealing a dislike of direct personal disclosure that is similar to Dr. Johnson's: "The truth is, that, though we may be led to mention ourselves, it is ever a tedious task to write at length on the subject: recollections come by crowds; hopes baffled; our dearest memories discovered to have a taint, our lives wasted and fallen into contempt even in our own eyes: so that we readily turn from dispiriting realities to such creatures of the imagination as we can fashion according to our liking" (III, 133).

Even this expressed preference for dealing with "creatures of the imagination," rather than with autobiographical material, receives significant qualification by 1843. "You asked me about writing," Mary wrote to Edward Moxon on September 20, "Is it a novel or a romance you want?—I should prefer quieter work, to be gathered from other works—such as my lives for the Cyclopedia—& which I think I do *much* better than romancing."[30] In short, Mary's extensive interest in biography probably reflects a deeper faith in a social reality outside herself than many of her greater contemporaries were able to muster in the context of early nineteenth-century

Europe—although the most notable exceptions, Scott and Jane Austen, are surely helpful for suggesting the often contradictory position that Mary Shelley held in the literature of the age.

The first we hear of the ambitious biographical project Mary undertook in the 1830's—The *Lives* in the *Cabinet Cyclopedia*—occurs in a letter to Maria Gisborne of July 17, 1834: "I am engaged writing the Lives of some of the Italian Literati for Dr. Lardner's Cyclopedia—I have written those of Petrarch Boccaccio &c and am now engaged on Machiavelli.—This takes up my time and is a source of interest and pleasure."[31] Six months later, on February 1, 1835, the first volume of Italian *Lives* appeared, and it was followed by a second in October. Then, in 1837, the initial project—*Lives of the Most Eminent Literary and Scientific Men of Italy, Spain and Portugal*—reached completion with the publication of a third volume, dealing with Spanish and Portuguese writers. (In the *Cabinet Cyclopedia* the volumes are numbered 63, 71, and 96, respectively.) But, although the three volumes totaled over one thousand pages (most of them written by Mary herself), she was already at work by early 1837 on a fresh assignment for the general editor of the series, the Reverend Dionysius Lardner—the researching and writing of two volumes of French *Lives* which, when published in 1838 and 1839, totaled over seven hundred pages.[32] (Their numbers in the *Cabinet Cyclopedia* are 105 and 117.)

More specifically, the Italian *Lives* range from Dante (1265–1321) to Ugo Foscolo (1778–1827). Approximately thirty figures are considered in the two volumes, some receiving only a few lines of assessment (Bernardo Pulci, Luca Pulci [I, 167]); but others receive biographical and critical attention which runs to over sixty pages. Of the ones receiving fairly detailed treatment, there are twelve: five in the first volume (Dante, Petrarch, Boccaccio, Ariosto, Machiavelli), seven in the second (Galileo, Torquato Tasso, Metastasio, Goldoni, Alfieri, Monti, Ugo Foscolo). Of these twelve, however, only eight are Mary's. The sketches of Dante, Ariosto, and Tasso belong to James Montgomery; the one of Galileo, to Sir David Brewster.[33] Furthermore, it is of some interest to note that, aside from Brewster's "Galileo" (II, 1–62), the only figures treated in the Italian *Lives* are those who gained eminence through their literary activities. Indeed, Galileo and, to a much more qualified degree, Pascal in the first volume of the French *Lives* are the only two men of science treated throughout the entire five volumes of biographical sketches, so that the title given in common to all—*Lives of the Most Eminent Literary and Scientific Men . . .*—is surely something of a misnomer. (Whether this fact made Lardner unhappy is something which is now impossible to know; but he was himself a man of wide, if hardly profound, scientific knowledge; and the volumes in the *Cabinet Cyclopedia* on hydrostatics and pneumatics [no. 17], on heat [no. 39], on arithmetic [no. 55], and on geometry [no. 127] are all from his own pen.)

The volume on Spanish and Portuguese *Lives* is divided into two unequal parts. The first, and by far the longer, opens with a historical survey of the beginnings of Spanish literature, treats more than twenty figures at varying length (the longest study, nearly seventy pages, is of Cervantes), and closes with a brief consideration of Calderón (1600–1681). The second part of the volume consists of only two sections: a seven-page survey of the predecessors of Camoëns, entitled "The Early Poets of Portugal" (Ribeyra, Sá de Miranda, Gil Vicente, Ferreira), and an almost forty-page discussion of Camöens himself (1524–80). Aside from Camoëns and Cervantes, the figures who receive relatively full consideration in this volume are Boscán, Garcilaso de la Vega, Ercilla, Lope de Vega, and Quevedo. Only the essay on Ercilla seems to be by another hand than Mary's.[34]

The two volumes of French *Lives* range from Rabelais (1494–1553) to Madame de Staël (1766–1817). Altogether, seventeen figures are treated: eleven in the first volume (Montaigne, Rabelais, Corneille, La Rochefoucauld, Molière, La Fontaine, Pascal, Madame de Sévigné, Boileau, Racine, Fénelon); six in the second (Voltaire, Rousseau, Condorcet, Mirabeau, Madame Roland, Madame de Staël). Of the sketches, the longest by far is the one devoted to Voltaire, which comprises over a hundred pages (II, 1–110). Interestingly enough, however, the preponderance of space in the treatment of Voltaire—Rousseau, for example, receives less than seventy pages—is hardly matched by the level of esteem. Mary writes of Voltaire in one of her better-turned and near-Johnsonian sentences, "He was, it is true, of the second order of minds, but first among the second; and such was his perfection in his art, as far as it went, that he contrived, while living, to fill out a first place, and will always receive a larger share of attention and praise than his intrinsic merits deserve" (II, 110).

Obviously, too, for one reason or another (and perhaps Mary's experience with the earlier, three-volume project is the true answer), the sketches in the French *Lives* reflect a more nearly equitable distribution of attention from one figure to the next. Thus the shortest "life" in the French series is the seventeen-page essay devoted to Rabelais (I, 23–29), and no other "life" falls below twenty pages. Yet in the Italian *Lives* at least fifteen figures are treated in discussions of less than ten pages apiece; and in the Spanish and Portuguese *Lives* an even greater diffusion of treatment is found.

Of more general considerations, three points seem worth making about the *Lives* as a whole. The first is that Mary's opportunity to write them reflects how high her reputation actually was in her own time. Of the thirty-eight authors listed in the "Analytical Catalogue" of the *Cabinet Cyclopedia*, she is the only woman. Furthermore, although Thackeray might satirize the general editor as "Dionysius Diddler" and suggest he was nothing but a literary quack, Lardner possessed an unusually shrewd mind, as well as, evidently, a remarkably persuasive manner. Some of the most notable writers of the period are numbered among the contributors to the *Cabinet Cyclopedia*—Scott, for example, was the author of the two-volume history of Scotland; Thomas Moore wrote the four-volume history of Ireland; Sismondi, perhaps the greatest living European historian, contributed three volumes (nos. 27, 56, 61); Dr. Thirlwall prepared the eight-volume history of Greece; Southey, still of course the poet laureate, contributed four volumes on the lives of British naval commanders; Sir James Mackintosh was the major contributor to the ten-volume history of England; and John Forster was the author of the five volumes of lives of British statesmen. In short, Mary's presence among the contributors to Lardner's scheme should be recognized as the distinction it was. The *Cabinet Cyclopedia* may have risen only rarely above the level of the semipopularization that was its major purpose; all the same, to be one of the writers—"hacks" would be unjust—in Dr. Lardner's stable was to find oneself in some very distinguished company indeed.

A second point worth making about the *Lives* is the general competence of the style throughout. Consistently intelligent, often effectively epigrammatic, occasionally personal and autobiographic, and only rarely sentimental, Mary's writing in sketch after sketch maintains itself at a much higher average level than the distracting unevenness which we find some years later in the *Rambles*. At times, it is true, Mary descends into the ignorant generalizations of her period—as in this comment from the sketch of Corneille: "It has been remarked that the sublimest passages of our greatest poets are written in *short words,* that is, in Anglo-Saxon, or pure English" (I, 61). Again, as I have already indicated, Mary occasionally ventures into autobiographic allusion; and, having made the gesture, she is not able to resist indulging in a sentimental outburst—although, as in a passage growing out of Madame de La Fayette's grief over the death of La Rochefoucauld, the sentimentality is shot through with an interesting suggestion of what may have been one of the major reasons behind Mary's refusal to marry again:

> These are the stings, this the poison, of death. There is no recall for a hasty word; no excuse, no pardon, no forgetfulness, for injustice or neglect;—the grave that has closed over the living form, and blocked up the future, causes the past to be indelible; and, as human weakness for ever errs, here it finds the punishment of its errors. While we love, let us ever remember that the loved one may die,—that we ourselves may die. Let all be true and open, let all be faithful and single-hearted, or the poison-harvest reaped after death may infect with pain and agony one's life of memory. (I, 91)

But, against these infrequent lapses into the tone of the inferior fiction Mary was writing in the same decade, we must set passage after passage of intelligent, well-turned prose—such as this paragraph, which concludes the study of La Rochefoucauld:

> Besides the maxims, Rochefoucauld wrote memoirs of various periods of the regency of Anne of Austria and the wars of the Fronde. Bayle bestows great encomium on this work: "I am sure," he says, "there are few partisans of antiquity who will not set a higher value on the duke de la Rochefoucauld's memoirs than on Caesar's commentaries." To which remark the only reply must be, that Bayle was better able to dissect motives, appreciate actions, and reason on truth and falsehood, than to discover the merit of a literary work. . . . The chief fault of the memoirs is the subject of them,—the wars of the Fronde,—a period of history distinguished by no men of exalted excellence; neither adorned by admirable actions nor conducing to any amelioration in the state of society: it was a war of knaves (not fools) for their own advancement, ending in their deserved defeat. (I, 96)

Or, to move into the Italian *Lives,* the sentence which begins the sketch of Machiavelli (it might almost be the opening of one of Johnson's essays) displays the balance and quiet force that led many of Mary's contemporaries to call her style "masculine": "There is no more delightful literary task than the justifying a hero or writer, who has been misrepresented and reviled; but such is human nature, or such is the small progress that we have made in the knowledge of it, that in most instances we excuse, rather than exculpate, and display doubts instead of bringing forward certainties" (I, 256). Altogether, then, the style of the *Lives* well deserves the praise several twentieth-century critics have bestowed on it—most notably perhaps Sylva Norman, who has found in the sketches for the *Cabinet Cyclopedia* Mary's "soundest, most scholarly and efficient writing."[35]

The third and final point about the *Lives* as a whole is that the critical judgments in them occasionally seem to be influenced unduly by what Mary likes to call "ideality"—and Byron "cant." Thus, Petrarch (Teresa Guiccioli's favorite poet, it might be pointed out) receives from Mary a much higher mark in relation to Dante than anyone today would be tempted to give him: "There is more refinement in Petrarch, and more elegance of versification, but scarcely more grace of expression" (I, 106). And it is, of course, Petrarch's poetry concerning Laura that most moves Mary—the hopelessness of the passion celebrated in it, the "ideality," the thoroughgoing fidelity: "[Laura] was distinguished by her rank and fortune, but more by her loveliness, her sweetness, and the untainted purity of her life and manners in the midst of a society noted for its licentiousness. Now she is known as the subject of Petrarch's verses; as the woman who inspired an immortal passion, and, kindling into living fire the dormant sensibility of the poet, gave origin to the most beautiful and refined, the most passionate, and yet the most delicate, amatory poetry that exists in the world" (I, 69).

A writer like Rabelais, on the other hand, fares rather badly by the standards of "ideality": "His great and fatal blemish is his grossness, his disregard of all decency, his sympathy with nastiness, his invasion of all this is weak and vile in the recesses of nature and the imagination" (I, 36). And this standard of judgment leads Mary at times into the rather unattractive strictures of prudery: "The tone of *Candide* is not moral, and, like all Voltaire's lighter

productions, is stamped with a coarseness which renders it unfit
for general perusal" (II, 77). "The second fault of [La Fontaine's]
tales, their licentiousness, is unpardonable" (I, 180). "Worse for
the fame of Boccaccio than the blots that slur the beauty of the
Decameron, is a work, which it is to be lamented fell from his pen.
This was entitled the *Corbaccio,* [written] . . . in a style that prevents
any one of the present day from attempting to read it" (I, 135).
In short, although the intelligence displayed in the *Lives* is consistently high, the critical standards which underlie many of the
incidental judgments—and, perhaps, a few of the central ones—
reflect that profound revolution in taste to which we have given
the convenient, if grossly oversimplified, label of Victorianism.

   In summary, the sketches for the *Cabinet Cyclopedia* represent
Mary at her most solid and substantial in the years after *The Last
Man.* Indeed, when we to come to the *Lives* after a reading of *Lodore,
Falkner,* and the short stories, we discover again the depressing
truth that a high intelligence may exist simultaneously with creative
debility. And perhaps Mary Shelley reveals, in her own smaller
way, the instinctive wisdom found in the careers of Matthew Arnold
and E. M. Forster: when a genuinely creative drive is no longer
present, the wisest use of a man's skills may lie in a concentration
upon "humbler" modes of expression, such as the critical and the
biographical. Mary herself, of course, failed to arrive completely at
such a conclusion; but, in comparison to some of the greater figures
of the nineteenth century (Wordsworth and Browning, for example,
with their long dreary wastes of later poetry), she does demonstrate,
through her *Lives,* the possibility that the choice of a less ambitious
form of literature may result paradoxically in a higher level of
achievement.

III *Mary and Shelley*

   For one reason or another—perhaps because of the tendency
of the eminent to attract gossip; perhaps because of the formidable
nature of the poetry itself—Shelley has always drawn an inordinate
amount of attention with respect to his private, and especially
his sexual, life. Did he, or did he not, have an affair with Claire
Clairmont? If so, where was it? In England? Italy? Both? (Reading
through the fringes of Shelley "scholarship," we are occasionally
driven to wonder whether some of the commentators have any

interest at all in his poetry.) And what about Harriet Shelley? Was she actually pregnant with Shelley's own child when she drowned herself? Or what about Elise, the Shelley's nursemaid? Is she the secret mother of Shelley's "Neapolitan charge"? (The list, like Banquo's issue, could easily be extended.)

And, of course, Mary herself, as Shelley's intimate companion for the last eight years of his life, has drawn a goodly share of this same sort of attention. Was she a good wife to Shelley? Did she *really* go to bed with Thomas Jefferson Hogg? Was Shelley driven into despair by her failure—for that matter, was Mary driven into despair by *his* failure—to understand his *(her)* physical and emotional needs? Wisely or not, such questions are unexplored in this section.[36] Rather, the primary interest is in two less dramatic aspects of Mary's relationship to Shelley: her editing of his poetry and prose; and the nature of her prefaces and notes to the various editions.

In essence, Mary's editing of Shelley's poetry and prose may be discussed on the basis of four separate editions: (1) *Posthumous Poems of Percy Bysshe Shelley* (1824); (2) the four volumes of *The Poetical Works of Percy Bysshe Shelley* (1839); (3) the one-volume but enlarged *The Poetical Works of Percy Bysshe Shelley* (1839); and (4) the two-volume *Essays, Letters from Abroad, Translations and Fragments* (1839, dated 1840). In the *Posthumous Poems,* a number of works appeared in print for the first time, including "Julian and Maddalo," "The Witch of Atlas," "Letter to Maria Gisborne," and "The Triumph of Life." In the next two editions, those of 1839, Mary provided the nucleus for all subsequent "complete" editions of Shelley's poetry. And, in the fourth, Mary's edition of the prose, she published a number of Shelley's essays for the first time, placing particular emphasis on "A Defence of Poetry," as well as introducing into print a collection of Shelley's letters but confining herself to a selection of those written from abroad.

Of the quality of the labor expended on these editions a good deal has recently been said, and a brief enumeration of Mary's editorial shortcomings probably makes clear the reason for these commentaries. First of all, by twentieth-century standards, she was woefully remiss as an editor. As Joseph Raben has damningly remarked in an article published in 1966, "Mary in her role of editor manipulated the raw materials of Shelley's notebooks.... Not only with the 'Invocation [to Misery],' but with other posthumous poems as

well, she emended, altered, misdated, and suppressed while at the
same time proclaiming her fidelity to the manuscripts."[37] Second,
aside from those specific failings of commission, Mary was also
guilty, in the four-volume edition of *The Poetical Works* of 1839,[38]
of a glaring error of omission. Confronted with the task of submitting
copy to the printer but reluctant to allow precious first editions to
go out of her hands, Mary compromised by forwarding to Moxon
secondary editions of Shelley's poetry—the Galignani edition
of 1828 and the two volumes published by John Ascham in 1834.

Consequently, as Charles H. Taylor, Jr., has shown with scholarly
thoroughness and authority, the text of Shelley's poetry, as Moxon
first published it in 1839, suffers from a host of corruptions introduced after Shelley's death: Volumes I, III, and IV have as their
basis the text of Ascham's edition; Volume II is essentially based on
Galignani's edition.[39] Fortunately, despite Professor Taylor's
implications to the contrary, very few of these corruptions have
survived into the twentieth century; and, as a partial explanation
for Mary's laxity with the 1839 editions, it might be pointed out—as
indeed Professor Taylor has—that her labors were far more sustained in editing the *Posthumous Poems* (on which a significant
part of the secondary editions were based)[40]—and that, furthermore, she played an important role in the construction of the expanded text of the Galignani edition.[41]

Two serious faults Mary had as an editor, then, were her extreme
carelessness at times about establishing the most accurate text and
her suppression of material which, for one reason or another, she
did not wish to bring before the public eye. For example, "Lines
Written during the Castlereagh Administration" was not published
in the *Posthumous Poems;* parts of *Queen Mab,* as well as all of
Peter Bell the Third and of *Swellfoot the Tyrant* failed to appear in
the first edition of 1839; both "A Philosophical View of Reform"
and an "Essay on the Devil and Devils" remained unpublished
during Mary's lifetime. Last of all, and perhaps most seriously,
Mary did not hesitate to manipulate the text itself, either for the
sake of what she apparently felt to be "improvement" or for the
purpose of concealing something unpleasant or embarrassing.[42]

Without attempting to disguise her failings, however, surely
something more positive can be said about her editorial labors
than many recent critics have been willing to allow. For one thing,
it seems rather unrealistic to hold Mary Shelley to the editorial

standards of our own time. Arbitrary manipulations similar to Mary's were fairly common in the nineteenth century,[43] and we would perhaps do well to remember that our current insistence on absolute textual fidelity is a partial outgrowth of the loss of any general audience for poetry. Indeed, and somewhat ironically, one of the most distinguished editions of a Shelley poem ever published in this country—Donald H. Reiman's *Shelley's "The Triumph of Life"* (1965)—has not escaped criticism from England for its being *excessively* faithful to Shelley's imperfect text.[44]

Another extenuating factor is the extreme difficulty of the task which confronted Mary. No one who has worked with Shelley's manuscripts has ever disputed the fundamental accuracy of Trelawny's description of one of them:

> The day I found Shelley in the pine forest he was writing verses. . . . I picked up a fragment, but could only make out the first two lines:
>
> > *Ariel, to Miranda take*
> > *This slave of music.*
>
> It was a frightful scrawl; words smeared out with his finger, and one upon the other, over and over in tiers, and all run together in most "admired disorder"; it might have been taken for a sketch of a marsh overgrown with bulrushes, and the blots for wild ducks.[45]

And Mary not only confirms this description but underscores the magnitude of her own undertaking: "Did any one see the papers from which I drew that volume," she writes of the *Posthumous Poems*, "the wonder would be how any eyes or patience were capable of extracting it from so confused a mass, interlined and broken into fragments, so that the sense could only be deciphered and joined by guesses which might seem rather intuitive than founded on reasoning."[46]

Furthermore, in neither period of her major editorial labors was Mary in a state of mind conducive to dispassionate, thoroughgoing accuracy. In 1822–24, she was oppressed on all sides by severe emotional distractions—grief over Shelley's loss, a sense of guilt for her irritability with him in the last years of his life, profound uncertainty about the future of herself and her son, constant financial worries, rude and unsympathetic treatment from Sir Timothy, and apprehension about, and then excessive concern for, the nature of her position in English society. Nor was her condition in the second half of the 1830's much superior; for, never too robust in health, Mary found that working with Shelley's manuscripts produced in her an intense and debilitating reaction. On February 12, 1839, for example, she wrote in her journal: "I almost think that my present occupation will end in a fit of illness. I am editing Shelley's Poems, and writing notes for them. . . . I am torn to pieces by memory."[47] A month later she wrote: "Illness did ensue. What an illness! driving me to the verge of insanity. Often I felt the cord would snap, and I should no longer be able to rule my thoughts; with fearful struggles, miserable relapses, after long repose, I became somewhat better."[48]

And this emotional and physical toll was so pronounced that, in the notes to the poems of 1822, Mary specifically apologized both to the reader and to Shelley's memory for the deficiencies of her performance: "I began with energy, and a burning desire to impart to the world, in worthy language, the sense I have of the virtues and genius of the beloved and the lost; my strength has failed under the task. Recurrence to the past, full of its own deep and unforgotten joys and sorrow, contrasted with succeeding years of painful and solitary struggle, has shaken my health. Days of great suffering have followed my attempts to write, and these again produced a weakness and languor" (Shelley, *Poems,* 675).

Altogether, then, Mary should be judged as an editor by a standard somewhat broader than that of today's academic "perfection." By her own lights—and the editorial lights of her generation—she was often conscientious to a praiseworthy degree.[49] Often, too, her distortions and suppression apparently grew out of nothing more sinister than a desire that Shelley's writings be as "popular" as possible.[50] Indeed, one of the least attractive things about some of her critics is their inability to remember that at the time of Mary's most strenuous editorial labors—on the *Posthumous Poems*—there were few people in England who believed Shelley worthy of any trouble at all.

And perhaps it is not inappropriate to conclude this brief assessment of Mary as Shelley's editor with a paraphrase from the writer who became an especial favorite of hers in her later years, Dr. Johnson: "In this work, when it shall be found that much is omitted, let it not be forgotten that much likewise is performed, and, though no edition was ever spared out of tenderness to the editor, and the world is little solicitous to know whence proceeded the faults of that which it condemns, yet it may gratify curiosity to inform it that the labor was performed with little assistance of the learned, and without any patronage of the great; not in the soft obscurities of retirement, or under the shelter of academic bowers, but amidst inconvenience and distraction, in sickness and in sorrow."

IV *The Prefaces and Notes*

Altogether, Mary wrote three separate prefaces to Shelley's work—one each for the edition of the *Posthumous Poems,* for the four-volume edition of poetry of 1839, and for the two-volume edition of the prose of 1840—as well as a brief prefatory postscript to the second edition of the poetry in 1839. In addition, she wrote a number of illustrative and explanatory notes, the most signifi-cant and substantial of which are those included in the two editions of poetry of 1839. As employed by most critics, however, the term "notes" is usually meant to imply all of Mary's commentary on Shelley in the four editions, including the three prefaces and the postscript.

The general critical problem presented by these notes may perhaps be made clear by the citation of two commentators—Herbert Read and Sylva Norman. For Read, Mary's notes are ultimately respon-sible for that nineteenth-century emasculation of Shelley that was given its most famous—or notorious—expression in Matthew Arnold's dismissal of the poet as a "beautiful and ineffectual angel." Thus Read writes: "Inept as Arnold was, the real villain of the piece is Mary Shelley, who, however difficult she may have found her husband in life, did nothing but sentimentalize him in death. It was she who, in the notes she affixed to the posthumous edition of his Poems, created the image of a whimsy Ariel which has ever since been so dear to superficial critics and romantic biographers."[51]

For Sylva Norman, on the other hand, the notes provide an invaluable "clue" to an understanding of Shelley's poetry, as well as representing, in their own right, a considerable literary achieve-ment: "Mary's notes everywhere supply a biographical and spiritual clue to the poems, besides rendering Shelley's tragedy forever inseparable from his writings. The sympathy and intense emotion that drove her pen have given them a quality that is, on its own note, almost as lasting and unforgettable as the poetry itself. In this work

Mary, without fictional barriers, wrote with deep sincerity and touched her zenith. However we may judge her other writings, it is these editorial notes which, appearing in the later 'definitive' editions of the poems, establish her place in literature."[52]

The existence of such a pronounced divergence of opinion quite clearly suggests a central difficulty in reaching a just estimate of Mary's notes. To approach them as Read does, with an eye to their deficiencies, is to see readily enough where Mary failed. For one thing, as he argues, she does indeed sentimentalize Shelley. In her conclusion to the note on *The Witch of Atlas,* for example, she presents a picture of an extraordinarily timid poet: "Shelley shrunk instinctively from portraying human passion, with its mixture of good and evil, of disappointment and disquiet. Such opened again the wound of his own heart; and he loved to shelter himself rather in the airiest flights of fancy, forgetting love and hate, and regret and lost hope, in such imaginations as borrowed their hues from sunrise or sunset, from the yellow moonshine or paly twilight, from the aspect of the far ocean or the shadows of the woods" (Shelley, *Poems,* 289).

Again, near the end of her long note on *Prometheus Unbound,* Mary creates a personality very different from the one who wrote the bitter invective found in "To the Lord Chancellor,"[53] in "The Mask of Anarchy," and in stanzas xxviii–xxix, xxxvi–xxxvii of *Adonais:* "An exile, and strongly impressed with the feeling that the majority of his countrymen regarded him with sentiments of aversion such as his own heart could experience towards none . . ." (Shelley, *Poems,* 274). Still again, in her preface to the two-volume edition of the prose of 1840, Mary depicts a Shelley remarkably akin to her sentimental portrayal of Rousseau in the French *Lives* only one year earlier—as the juxtaposition of the two passages demonstrates:

Shelley's own definition of Love follows; and reveals the secrets of the most impassioned, and yet the purest and softest heart that ever yearned for sympathy, and was ready to give its own, in lavish measure, in return. (I, x)

He [Rousseau] felt it in his own person, when his unguarded and softened heart was suddenly possessed by a passion the most vehement and unfortunate that ever caused a frail human being to thrill and mourn. (II, 141)

For another thing, this tendency to sentimentalize Shelley produces (although Read exaggerates in this respect) its occasional "spiritual" consequence: the etherealization of Shelley. Thus, in her preface to the first edition of 1839, Mary writes: "Whatever faults he had ought to find extenuation among his fellows, since they prove him to be human; without them, the exalted nature of his soul would have raised him into something divine" (Shelley, *Poems,* ix). And in the note to *Queen Mab,* she remarks of his entrance into Eton: "Inspired with ardour for the acquisition of knowledge, endowed with the keenest sensibility and with the fortitude of a martyr, Shelley came among his fellow creatures, congregated for the purposes of education, like a spirit from another sphere" (Shelley, *Poems,* 835). But such passages are relatively rare in the notes, and seems rather disingenuous of Read to shift to Mary both the guilt and the explanation for one of the major critical problems of English "Romantic" poetry—the extraordinary range of reactions Shelley has elicited from distinguished critics.

Far more important is the tendency Mary exhibits in the notes of unconsciously quarreling with Shelley for not having been another kind of poet. And this aspect, in turn, is closely related to a point made somewhat earlier (see Chapter 5, Section III) in the brief discussion of Mary's verse: that her deepest sympathies actually lay with the "lesser" Shelley—with the creator of the over-anthologized lyrics and of a good deal of greatly inferior poetry. (It is surely no accident that Shelley finished *Rosalind and Helen* at Mary's specific request.) Thus, in the preface to the first edition of 1839, in a passing reference to the tragedy of Shelley's early death (a tragedy to which she recurs in similar fashion throughout the notes), Mary writes in a way that almost compels the conclusion that, if Shelley had written a different kind of poetry, Mary would have been a happier woman: "It must be remembered that there is the stamp of . . . inexperience on all he wrote; he had not completed his nine-and-twentieth year when he died. The calm of middle life did not add the seal of virtues which adorn maturity to those generated by the vehement spirit of youth" (Shelley, *Poems,* xi).

And this "different" kind of poetry that Mary truly wanted Shelley to write can be described—if a little unfairly—by the adjective "popular." Certainly, at any rate, Mary herself resorts to this adjective with fairly regular frequency. "His success," Mary writes of *The Cenci,* "was a double triumph; and often after he was ear-

nestly entreated [obviously by Mary] to write again in a style that
commanded popular favour. . . . But the bent of his mind went the
other way" (Shelley, *Poems,* 337). "I felt sure," she writes in her
note to *The Witch of Atlas,* "that, if his poems were more addressed
to the common feelings of men, his proper rank among the writers
of the day would be acknowledged, and that popularity as a poet
would enable his countrymen to do justice to his character and
virtues" (Shelley, *Poems,* 388). And in the preface to the first edition of 1839, there is a hint of vexation at Shelley's having remained
so obstinate a poet in his own lifetime:

> The metaphysical strain that characterizes much of what he has written
> was, indeed, the portion of his works to which, apart from those whose
> scope was to awaken mankind to aspirations for what he considered the
> true and good, he was himself particularly attached. There is much, however,
> that speaks to the many. When he would consent to dismiss these huntings
> after the obscure (which, entwined with his nature as they were, he did with
> difficulty), no poet ever expressed in sweeter, more heart-reaching, or more
> passionate verse, the gentler or more forcible emotions of the soul. (Shelley,
> *Poems,* xi)

But, despite this enumeration of the deficiencies (which is far from
complete), there is much evidence to be cited in support of Sylva
Norman's favorable assessment of the notes. Thus, in her comments
on *The Revolt of Islam,* Mary makes a general critical statement
about the quality of Shelley's mind which Read himself—somewhat
contradictorily, one might think—calls the "truest" thing ever
written about Shelley:[54] "Shelley possessed two remarkable
qualities of intellect—a brilliant imagination, and a logical exactness
of reason" (Shelley, *Poems,* 156). Again, in a passage about the life
the two of them lived at Marlow, Mary presents a picture of Shelley
which is neither sentimental nor ethereal; and she expresses it in
a tone which catches something of Shelley's own generous indig-
nation at social injustice:

> With all this wealth of Nature which, either in the form of gentlemen's
> parks or soil dedicated to agriculture, flourishes around, Marlow was
> inhabited (I hope it is altered now) by a very poor population. There women
> are lacemakers, and lose their health by sedentary labour, for which
> they were very ill paid. The Poor-laws ground to the dust not only the
> paupers, but those who had risen just above that state, and were obliged
> to pay poor-rates. The changes produced by peace following a long war,
> and a bad harvest, brought with them the most heart-rending evils to the

poor. Shelley afforded what alleviation he could. In the winter, while bringing out his poem [*The Revolt of Islam*], he had a severe attack of oph- thalmia, caught while visiting the poor cottages. I mention these things— for this minute and active sympathy with his fellow-creatures gives a thousandfold interest to his speculations, and stamps with reality his pleadings for the human race. (Shelley, *Poems,* 157)

Still again, Mary is not averse to mentioning an aspect of Shelley that the nineteenth century rarely chose to recognize—his Marxian anticipations: "Shelley loved the People; and respected them as often more virtuous, as always more suffering, and therefore more deserving of sympathy, than the great. He believed that a clash between the two classes of society was inevitable, and he eagerly ranged himself on the people's side" (Shelley, *Poems,* 588).

Although a much longer list of citations favorable to Mary could be drawn from the notes, the general conclusion seems evident. Read with a jaundiced eye, Mary's commentary on Shelley is sentimental, limited in perception, and misdirected in its praise. Indeed, the commentaries sometimes appear to be an amplification of the spirit of Mary's comment to John Murray in 1830: "I have no pretensions to being a critic—yet I know infinitely well what pleases me."[55] But, when read with a willingness to allow Mary her liabilities, she emerges in the notes as a generous, often pas- sionately sincere, and occasionally quite perceptive commentator on her husband's poetry. In a century when Shelley was at times extremely unfortunate in his critics, such a score is hardly a disgrace- ful one.

Conclusion

"AH, did you once see *Mary* Shelley plain?"—Apparently, nobody ever did; for, in her own smaller way, the contradictions elicited by her personality have been almost as noticeably diverse as those generated by Shelley himself. Reviled by Trelawny while she was still alive and sentimentalized after her death by Mrs. Marshall in one of the earliest biographies, Mary has continued to receive a good deal of attention that is really more concerned about attacking or defending her character than in subjecting her writings to a genuine scrutiny.

The purpose of this study, then, has not been so much to see Mary Shelley "plain"—a perhaps futile task—but to explore the nature of her significance as a writer. Preeminently, it seems to me, that significance rests on her three early novels—*Frankenstein, The Last Man,* and *Valperga*—in that order. Indeed, such a total achievement ought to have earned for Mary a higher place in the literature about the fiction of the period than she currently holds. For, while Scott and Jane Austen are far superior to her, when we descend from these two, past Peacock, into the host of novelists who were Mary's contemporaries in the early nineteenth century, it is difficult to discover—on the basis of the seriousness of conception, the originality and variety of technique, and the relevance to their time and to our own—anything to equal the over-all implications of Mary's three novels.

Furthermore, although the remainder of her fiction, with the exception of *Mathilda,* is relatively unimportant, Mary's nonfiction can hardly be summarily dismissed. For one thing, the notes on Shelley will continue to receive attention—and deservedly so—for as long as the poet himself is studied. For another, although it would be foolish to claim for them the peculiar importance which the notes on Shelley possess, Mary's biographical sketches for Lardner's *Cabinet Cyclopedia*—as well as, to lesser extent, her *Rambles*—offer to the reader a genuinely pleasurable experience.

Finally, however, any study of Mary Shelley must end on a note of regret for her failure to fulfill her early promise. Few novelists have begun with a debut as auspicious as that of *Frankenstein*. No other novelist of her time combined such a promising beginning with so youthful an age. And, when we consider that *Frankenstein* was not an entirely isolated phenomenon in Mary's career, the regret can only grow sharper. For, whatever the final conclusion may be about the unevenness of *Valperga, The Last Man* in its sustained conception is surely a novel with its own independent significance. Briefly, then, the last word on Mary Shelley must be one of regret for her failure to make of her career a more impressive creative whole. And although the reason for the failure can be debated (see above, Chapter 4, Section VI), it is the failure itself which matters. Out of it, in fact, can be found the basis on which Mary Shelley takes her place in English literature as a minor figure.

Notes and References

Chapter One

1. Ford K. Brown, *The Life of William Godwin* (London, 1926), p. 82.
2. Ralph M. Wardle, *Mary Wollstonecraft* (Lawrence, Kansas, 1951), p. 168.
3. Cited in Wardle, p. 162.
4. See the account of Mary Wollstonecraft by Eleanor L. Nicholes (correcting Wardle at times) in Kenneth Neill Cameron, ed., *Shelley and His Circle* (Cambridge, Mass., 1961), I, 39–66.
5. William Godwin, *Memoirs of Mary Wollstonecraft* (New York, 1930), pp. 112–23. Further information on Mary Wollstonecraft's death may be found in Cameron, ed., *Shelley and His Circle,* I, 185–201.
6. Brown, pp. 203–4.
7. Most probably Godwin was her first husband. See Herbert Huscher, "Charles Gaulis Clairmont," *Keats-Shelley Memorial Bulletin* VIII (1957), 11; Huscher, "The Clairmont Enigma," *Keats-Shelley Memorial Bulletin,* XI (1960), 14–15; Cameron, ed., *Shelley and His Circle,* I, 296–97, III, 374–75.
8. "Mary Shelley to Maria Gisborne: New Letters, 1818–1822," ed. Frederick L. Jones, *Studies in Philology,* LII (1955), 68 & n., 69.
9. *The Letters of Mary W. Shelley,* ed. Frederick L. Jones (Norman, 1946), I, 23. Hereafter cited as *Letters.*
10. *Letters,* I, 32.
11. Elizabeth Nitchie, *Mary Shelley* (New Brunswick, 1953), pp. 98–99.
12. *Lodore* (New York, 1835), pp. 57–58.
13. Far from being "illiterate," the second Mrs. Godwin took an active part in Godwin's publishing affairs, translating a number of children's books from French into English.
14. C. Kegan Paul, *William Godwin* (Boston, 1876), II, 108.
15. From an unpublished letter in Lord Abinger's collection, cited in Nitchie, *Mary Shelley,* p. 89.
16. *Letters,* II, 88.
17. See, for example, Mrs. Godwin's complaint to her husband, Aug. 14, 1811, less than a year before Mary's departure for Scotland: "in the hardest struggle that ever fell to the lot of a woman, I have lost my youth and beauty before the natural time" (Paul, II, 187).

18. Mary was under the care of a Mr. Cline for "a weakness in one arm" (Mrs. Julian Marshall, *Life of Mary Shelley* [London, 1889] I, 19).

19. Mrs. Marshall, I, 19.

20. Paul, II, 214.

21. *The Letters of Percy Bysshe Shelley,* ed. Frederick L. Jones (Oxford, 1964), I, 327 n. Hereafter cited as Shelley, *Letters.*

22. *Mathilda* (Chapel Hill, 1959), p. 8.

23. Author's Introduction (dated October 15, 1831), *Frankenstein.*

24. Shelley's entry, *Mary Shelley's Journal,* ed. Frederick L. Jones (Norman, 1947), p. 5. Hereafter cited as *Journal.*

25. *Journal,* p. 14.

26. Author's Introduction, *Frankenstein.*

27. See below, Chapter 2, sections II and III.

28. Mrs. Marshall, I, 66–67.

29. Author's Introduction, *Frankenstein.*

30. *Ibid.*

31. *Journal,* p. 5 & n. 3.

32. *Ibid.,* pp. 11–12. Shelley's title, however, did not have for him its present connotation of violence and murder.

33. *Journal,* p. 25.

34. Author's Introduction, *Frankenstein.*

35. *Journal,* pp. 40–41. See also her moving letter to Thomas Jefferson Hogg, March 6, 1815, *Shelley and His Circle,* III, 453.

36. The *History* was published in December, 1817. Since even the early part was based on the journal entries of both Shelley and Mary, it is clear that the *History,* in the strictest sense of the word, was a collaborative effort throughout. Indeed, Mary published a revised version of the *History* as part of her 1840 edition of Shelley's prose. For some interesting sidelights from Claire Clairmont's point of view, see *Shelley and His Circle,* III, 342–52.

37. Leigh Hunt, on Shelley's suggestion, published a paragraph of Mary's in the *Examiner* on October 5, 1817. The paragraph, a criticism of William Cobbett, was drawn from Mary's letter to Shelley of September 30; and it represents her first appearance in print (*Letters,* I, 37, 41 & n.).

38. *Shelley and Mary,* eds. Sir Percy Shelley and Lady Jane Shelley (privately printed, 1882), I, 327.

39. *Letters,* I, 290–91.

40. Mrs. Marshall, I, 243. But see also *Journal,* p. 122 & n. 24, and R. Glynn Grylls, *Mary Shelley* (London, 1938), p. 273.

41. Grylls, *Mary Shelley,* p. 273.

42. June 27, 1819, *Letters,* I, 73.

43. September 24, 1819, *Letters,* I, 81.

44. See below, Chapter 4, Section I.

45. *Journal,* p. 180.

46. May 15, 1824, *Journal*, p. 193.

47. October 5, 1822, *Journal*, p. 181.

48. Walter S. Scott, ed., *New Shelley Letters* (New Haven, 1949), pp. 139–44.

49. *Letters*, I, 193.

50. *Ibid.*, 260.

51. *Ibid.*, 303; see also I, 264 n.

52. *Ibid.*, 303.

53. *Ibid.*, II, 218.

54. *Ibid.*, 359.

55. Grylls, *Mary Shelley*, p. 275.

Chapter Two

1. For example: Sylva Norman, "Mary Shelley: Novelist," *On Shelley* (London, 1938), p. 63; Grylls, *Mary Shelley*, p. 319; Muriel Spark, *Child of Light* (Hadleigh, 1951), p. 129; Nitchie, *Mary Shelley*, p. 148; Lionel Stevenson, *The English Novel: A Panorama* (Cambridge, Mass., 1960), pp. 205–6; Ian Jack, *Oxford History of English Literature: English Literature 1815–1832* (Oxford, 1963), pp. 243–45.

2. Mrs. Marshall, II, 69. Mary, of course, was only nineteen when she completed *Frankenstein*.

3. Mrs. Marshall, II, 312.

4. R. Glynn Grylls, *Claire Clairmont: Mother of Byron's Allegra* (London, 1939), p. 278.

5. *History of a Six Weeks' Tour* (London, 1817), p. 15. Claire Clairmont's journal is also now conveniently available in *The Journals of Claire Clairmont*, ed. Marion Kingston Stocking (Cambridge, Mass., 1968).

6. Edward Dowden, *Shelley* (London, 1886), II, 545–46.

7. She was christened Clara Mary Jane Clairmont. For the approximate dates of the name changes, see Lorraine Roberston, "The Journals and Notebooks of Claire Clairmont," *Keats-Shelley Memorial Bulletin*, IV (1952), 45.

8. 1832, *Journal*, p. 202.

9. Mrs. Marshall, II, 248.

10. Dowden, II, 549; *Letters*, I, 8; *Journal*, pp. 46–47.

11. They are reprinted in *The Letters and Journals of Lord Byron*, ed. Rowland E. Prothero, III (London, 1922), Appendix VII. See also George Paston and Peter Quennell, eds., *To Lord Byron* (London, 1939), pp. 203–59.

12. Paston and Quennell, p. 210.

13. Shelley, *Letters*, I, 450, 453.

14. *Ibid.*, I, 470–71.

15. See the two valuable articles of Ernest Lovell, Jr. (listed in the Selected Bibliography).

16. Paston and Quennell, pp. 207–11.

17. *Shelley and Mary,* I, 91. But compare Peacock's account in Humbert Wolfe, ed., *The Life of Percy Bysshe Shelley* (London, 1933), II, 341–43.

18. Mrs. Marshall, I, 117–18; see also n. 10, above.

19. Paston and Quennell, p. 208.

20. Grylls, *Clairmont,* pp. 62–64; Leslie Marchand, *Byron* (New York, 1957), II, 620–21.

21. *The Diary of Dr. John William Polidori,* ed. William Michael Rossetti (London, 1911), p. 99.

22. Thomas Moore, *Lord Byron* (London, 1830), II, 24. Mary was Moore's major source for the details of Byron's stay at Geneva.

23. Sometimes called (erroneously) Montalègre.

24. Author's Introduction, *Frankenstein.* Unless otherwise noted, all citations are from the 1831 edition. First published in 1818 in three volumes, *Frankenstein* appeared again in 1823 in two volumes at Godwin's instigation. This "second" edition has no textual authority. There is, however, in the Morgan Library (W25A), a copy of the first edition of *Frankenstein* with corrections and suggested revisions in Mary's hand. Because this particular copy was no longer available to Mary in 1831 when the true second edition of *Frankenstein* was being readied, many of the suggested changes were never incorporated into the text.

25. Thomas Moore, II, 31.

26. The fullest account of this rare volume may be found in James Rieger, "Dr. Polidori and the Genesis of Frankenstein," *Studies in English Literature,* III (1963), 465–66.

27. Thomas Moore, II, 31.

28. John William Polidori, *The Vampyre* (London, 1819), pp. xiv–xv; see also Byron to John Murray, May 15, 1819, *Letters and Journals,* IV, 298.

29. Polidori, *Diary,* p. 125.

30. *Ibid.,* pp. 123–24.

31. Rieger, "Dr. Polidori," pp. 467–69.

32. *Journal,* p. 184.

33. Shelley, *Letters,* II, 33 & n.; and see also Mrs. Marshall, I, 220–21.

34. *Frankenstein; or the Modern Prometheus,* 3 vols. (London, 1818), I, 97.

35. *Letters,* I, 14.

36. See also Nitchie, *Mary Shelley,* pp. 196–97, for Mary's habit of extensive revision, most specifically with *Frankenstein.*

37. *Journal,* p. 53.

38. *Ibid.,* p. 60.

39. *Ibid.,* pp. 64, 68–70.

40. *Ibid.,* pp. 77–78.

41. *Ibid.,* p. 78.

42. *Ibid.,* p.79.

43. *Ibid.,* p. 80.

44. *Letters,* I, 26.

45. Shelley, *Letters,* I, 549.

46. See, however, Professor Jones's argument that another publisher than Ollier's was involved in the rejection of early August (Shelley, *Letters,* I, 551 n.).

47. *Journal,* p. 84; Shelley, *Letters,* I, 553, 556.

48. *Quarterly Review* (January, 1818), cited in Grylls, *Mary Shelley,* p. 316. A valuable consideration of the most prominent reviews are found in Grylls's biography, pp. 315–18. See also Nitchie, *Mary Shelley,* pp. 145–46; and Shelley, *Letters,* II, 23 n.

49. *Edinburg Magazine* (March, 1818), cited in Grylls, *Mary Shelley,* p. 317.

50. Shelley, *Letters,* I, 590.

51. *Blackwood's Edinburgh Magazine* (March, 1818), reprinted in Scott, *The Miscellaneous Prose Works,* XVIII (Edinburgh, 1851), 267–69.

52. *Shelley and Mary,* I, 327.

53. The influence of Coleridge's *Ancient Mariner* is, of course, strongly felt in this portion of the novel. See, for example, Walton's second letter.

54. Letter 4, August 13 entry.

55. See M.A. Goldberg's valuable article, "Moral and Myth in Mrs. Shelley's *Frankenstein,*" *Keats-Shelley Journal,* VIII (Part I, 1959), 27–38.

56. Walton's conclusion, September 2 entry.

57. Several critics have pointed to the fact that *Frankenstein* and his creation are but parts of a single being. See Richard Church, *Mary Shelley* (London, 1928), pp. 52–54; Spark, *Child of Light,* p. 134; Lowry Nelson, Jr., "Night Thoughts on the Gothic Novel," *Yale Review,* LII (Winter, 1963), 247–48; Harold Bloom, "Afterword," *Frankenstein* (New York, 1965), p. 213.

58. The major faults of the novel are these: extremely shadowy characterization aside from the two central figures, a thorough sentimentality in the presentation of the cottagers (Chaps. 12–14), and an overuse of coincidence. See also Spark, *Child of Light,* p. 143.

59. Walton's conclusion, September 12 entry.

60. Quoted in Grylls, *Mary Shelley,* p. 317. Scott, too, expressed uneasiness at using the word "creation" in connection with Frankenstein's achievement (*Miscellaneous Prose,* XVIII, 257).

61. Walton's conclusion, August 26 entry.

62. Medwin, *Shelley,* ed. Forman (1913), pp. 160–61.

63. Peter L. Thorslev, Jr., *The Byronic Hero* (Minneapolis, 1962), pp. 123–24 (drawing upon the research of Samuel C. Chew). All the same, the Byron scholars may have underestimated a quite early (1814) Promethean analogue in Shelley's *The Assassins,* Chapter 3.

64. Raymond Trousson, it seems to me, underestimates the degree to

which *Frankenstein* departs from earlier treatments (including Byron's "Prometheus") of the Promethean theme (*Le Thème de Prométhée dans la Littérature Européenne* [Genéve, 1964], II, 305–6.

65. Afterword, p. 213.

66. Letter 4, August 19 entry.

67. For a somewhat different reading of Frankenstein's failure of love, see Bloom, Afterword, p. 217.

68. Shelley, *The Revolt of Islam*, V, li, 3.

69. Although the "Defence of Poetry" was written well after the completion of *Frankenstein*, the distinction Shelley draws in its opening paragraphs between the reason and the imagination seems an apt analogue to Victor Frankenstein's manner of analytically attempting to produce a synthesis—that is, in the "creation" he is imaginatively deficient.

70. Of the finding of sources there is no end. The interested student may also wish to consult Burton R. Pollin, "Philosophical and Literary Sources of *Frankenstein*," *Comparative Literature*, XVII (Spring, 1965), 97–108, where analogues are noted with Milton's *Paradise Lost*, Locke's *Essay Concerning Human Understanding*, and Ovid's *Metamorphoses*.

71. See Grylls, *Mary Shelley*, pp. 316–17.

72. A more detailed criticism of Satan is found in Shelley's "Essay on the Devil and Devils," *Shelley's Prose*, ed. David Lee Clark, 2nd ed. (Albuquerque, 1966), esp. p. 267.

73. *Journal*, p. 60.

74. *Ibid.*, pp. 68–69.

75. Shelley was also reading *Political Justice* aloud in November (*Journal*, pp. 69–70).

76. William Godwin, *Enquiry concerning Political Justice . . .*, ed. F. E. L. Priestley, 3 vols. (Toronto, 1946), I, 323–24. This passage appeared in all three editions of *Political Justice*.

77. See also Spark, *Child of Light*, pp. 135–36, and Bloom, Afterword, pp. 215–16.

78. *Shelley's Prose*, pp. 307–8.

79. Scott, *Miscellaneous Prose*, XVIII, 254.

80. William Godwin, *St. Leon: A Tale of the Sixteenth Century* (London, 1799), II, 7.

81. *Ibid.*, II, 210.

82. *Ibid.*, IV, 8.

83. Maria Vohl, *Die Erzählungen der Mary Shelley und ihre Urbilder* (Heidelberg, 1913), p. 30; translation mine.

Chapter Three

1. Ed. *Letters*, I, xxx.

2. Norman, "Mary Shelley: Novelist," p. 64; more recently, however.

Sylva Norman has found kinder words for *Valperga*, calling it "healthy, passionate romance," Cameron, ed., *Shelley and His Circle*, III, 418.

3. Grylls, *Mary Shelley*, p. 321.

4. Spark, *Child of Light*, p. 125.

5. Nitchie, *Mary Shelley*, pp. 205–6.

6. See, for example, Shelley's scattered comments on the book in Shelley, *Letters*, II, 245, 312, 324, 352–53.

7. Mrs. Marshall, II, 52.

8. *Letters*, I, 145.

9. Shelley, *Letters*, II, 365; *Journal*, pp. 159–61.

10. See above, Chapter 1, Section III.

11. Newman Ivey White, *Shelley* (New York, 1940), II, 36–50; Nitchie, *Mary Shelley*, pp. 211–12.

12. Spark, *Child of Light*, p. 125.

13. Cf. Mary's comment to Leigh Hunt, August 3, 1823, more than a year after Shelley's death: "After all *Valperga* is merely a book of promise, another landing place in the staircase I am climbing" (*Letters*, I, 243); and see also below, Chapter 5, Section I.

14. In December, 1819, Mary wrote to Maria Gisborne: "Study I cannot for I have no books & may not call simple reading study for Papa is continually saying & writing that to read one book without others beside you to which you may refer is mere child's work" (*Letters*, I, 91).

15. Shelley, *Letters*, II, 245.

16. *Letters*, I, 145.

17. *Valperga* (London, 1823), I, iii. I have used these editions of the works Mary refers to: (1) "The Life of Castruccio Castricani of Lucca," *The Works of Nicholas Machiavel*, trans. Ellis Farneworth, 4 vols. (London, 1775), II, 439–77; (2) J. C. L. Sismondi, *Histoire des Républiques Italiennes du Moyen Age*, 5th ed., 8 vols. (Brussels, 1838), especially vols. II and III; (3) Niccolò Tegrimi, "Vita Castruccii Antelminelli," *Rerum Italicarum Scriptores*, ed. Lodovico Antonio Muratori, XI (Milan, 1727), 1315–44; (4) Giovanni Villani, *Istorie Fiorente*, 8 vols. (Milan, 1802), especially vol. VI. In addition, Mary also quotes in her preface from Louis Moreri's *Grand Dictionnaire Historique*.

18. The phrase is taken from the review in *Blackwood's Edinburgh Magazine*, which described *Valperga* as "a most romantic fiction," XIII (March, 1823), 283.

19. *Ibid.*, p. 284.

20. *Journal*, pp. 115–16; *Letters*, I, 62; "Mary Shelley to Maria Gisborne: New Letters," p. 48. Shelley's own comment on Sismondi (in his notes to *Hellas*) is of interest; he calls the history "a book which has done much towards awakening the Italians to an imitation of their great ancestors" (Shelley, *Poems*, 478).

21. *Journal*, p. 131.

22. *Ibid.,* pp. 138–42, 145, 152–53. For the fourth number of *The Liberal,* Mary also wrote a brief consideration of "the dear, rambling, old fashioned pages of Giovanni Villani" (*Liberal,* II, 281–97).

23. *Journal,* p. 158.

24. Shelley, *Letters,* II, 117.

25. *Letters,* I, 150, 159; Shelley, *Letters,* II, 117, 312, 352–53, 365, 371; Maria Gisborne, *Shelley's Friends,* ed. Frederick L. Jones (Norman, 1951), pp. 73–75.

26. *Letters,* I, 159; Shelley, *Letters,* II, 382, 424.

27. Paul, II, 277.

28. Spark, *Child of Light,* p. 125.

29. Norman, "Mary Shelley: Novelist," p. 64.

30. Paul, II, 277.

31. Mrs. Marshall, II, 52.

32. Nitchie, *Mary Shelley,* p. 150.

33. *Blackwood's,* XIII, 283, 284, 293.

34. Nitchie, *Mary Shelley,* p. 150.

35. *Letters,* I, 224; and see also I, 255.

36. Mrs. Marshall, II, 84.

37. *Letters,* II, 144 (Jones gives this letter a conjectural date of December, 1839). Grylls, *Mary Shelley,* p. 182, claims that "*Valperga* had sold as well as *Frankenstein,*" but Mary's own comments—as well as the book's publishing history—would seem to disprove this statement. And see also Thomas Medwin, *The Life of Percy Bysshe Shelley* (London, 1913), p. 374.

38. *Letters,* I, 260.

39. Roger Ingpen, *Shelley in England* (Boston and New York, 1917), II, 573.

40. *Ibid.*

41. Ingpen, II, 549 n.

42. *Ibid.,* II, 559.

43. Like all of Mary's novels, *Valperga* was published anonymously. The actual authorship was, however, common knowledge; and even the *Blackwood's* review, favorable as it was, expressed distress at the ideas Mary had absorbed from her milieu.

44. For a copy of the publisher's bill, see Ingpen, II, 584 n.

45. Shelley, *Letters,* II, 353–54.

46. Mary chose to make Castruccio younger than the age given him in any of her sources, obviously for the purpose of increasing the "romantic" aspects of his relationship with Euthanasia and Beatrice. Sismondi would place Castruccio's year of birth at about 1281 (III, 94); Machiavelli at about 1284 (II, 477); Villani at about 1281 (VI, 121); and Tegrimi at about 1281 (XI, 1315–16, 1342).

47. *Blackwood's,* XIII, 284.

48. The significant point that the novel truly ends with Euthanasia's

death is also made by Helen Moore, *Mary Wollstonecraft Shelley* (Philadelphia, 1886), p. 279.

49. For an interesting discussion of Beatrice's relevance to *The Cenci* and of Mary's use of Sismondi for her religious background, see James Rieger, "Shelley's Paterin Beatrice," *Studies in Romanticism,* IV (Autumn, 1964–Summer, 1965), 169–84. Rieger perhaps underestimates the similarity of Beatrice's most intense religious outburst (*Valperga,* III, 43–51) to the monster's bitterness in *Frankenstein.*

50. Shelley, *The Revolt of Islam,* Canto I, xxvii–xxviii, xxxi.

51. "Liberty had never been more devotedly worshipped than in the republic of Florence" (*Valperga,* I, 29). Cf. "A Philosophical View of Reform," *Shelley's Prose,* p. 231: "Freedom had one citadel wherein it could find refuge from a world which was its enemy: Florence."

52. Shelley, "An Ode: Written October 1819, before the Spaniards Had Recovered Their Liberty."

53. *Letters,* I, 104. Cf. Shelley's "Ode to Liberty."

54. *Ibid.,* I, 113. Cf. Shelley's "Ode to Naples."

55. *Ibid.,* I, 98.

56. *Shelley and Mary,* I, 281–83.

57. See especially, in Shelley's ode, lines 69–90, 136–50. Euthanasia's remark, of course, is also related to a major concept in "A Defence of Poetry."

58. Mrs. Marshall, II, 266. Cf., for example, Euthanasia's outbreak, "Oh! could I even now pour forth in words . . . " (I, 204), to Shelley's "Ode to a Skylark."

59. Sismondi, III, 94; translation mine. Mary apparently drew on this passage for a brief account of Castruccio's character as Euthanasia sees it in *Valperga* (III, 14).

60. Possibly the change was due to the publisher since Godwin was still calling the book *Castruccio* in late 1822 (Marshall, II, 52); Medwin, never too accurate, believed Godwin was responsible (*Shelley,* p. 374).

61. Brian Wilkie, *Romantic Poets and Epic Tradition* (Madison and Milwaukee, 1965), pp. 20–21.

62. *Ibid.,* p. 139. By the time of *Prometheus Unbound* (1819–20), of course, even the military metaphor has vanished from Shelley's concept of genuine heroism.

63. Machiavelli, trans. Farneworth, II, 441–42, 477.

64. "Mary Shelley to Maria Gisborne: New Letters," *Studies in Philology,* LII (1955), 55.

65. *Shelley's Prose,* p. 236. Other references to Napoleon by Shelley may be found in the following four poems: (1) "Feelings of a Republican on the Fall of Bonaparte," (2) "Lines Written on Hearing the News of the Death of Napoleon," (3) "Ode to Liberty" (Stanza XII), and (4) "The Triumph of Life" (ll. 215–234).

66. *Lives of . . . France*, II (London, 1839), 183.

67. *Lives of . . . Italy, Spain, and Portugal*, II (London, 1835), 367.

Chapter Four

1. Mary Shelley, *Tales and Stories*, ed. Richard Garnett (London, 1891), pp. vii–ix.

2. Jones, ed., *Letters*, I, xxx; White, *Shelley*, II, 386.

3. Grylls, *Mary Shelley*, p. 321.

4. Spark, *Child of Light*, pp. 1–2.

5. Nitchie, *Mary Shelley*, p. 153.

6. *The Last Man*, ed. Hugh J. Luke, Jr. (Lincoln, Nebraska, 1965). All citations from *The Last Man* are drawn from this edition.

7. *Keats-Shelley Journal*, XVI (1967), 109.

8. Walter Guzzardi, Jr., *Saturday Review*, XLIX, Part I (January–June, 1966), 86.

9. *College English*, XXVII (October, 1965–May, 1966), 646.

10. Quoted in Ingpen, II, 546.

11. See Lady Anne Hill, "Trelawny's Family Background and Naval Career," *Keats-Shelley Journal*, V (1956), 11–32; and cf. Leslie A. Marchand, "Trelawny on the Death of Shelley," *Keats-Shelley Memorial Bulletin*, IV (1952), 9–34.

12. Wolfe, II, 218.

13. *Letters*, I, 183.

14. *Ibid.*, I, 189.

15. *Ibid.*, I, 178.

16. *Ibid.*, I, 186.

17. *Ibid.*, I, 191–92.

18. *Ibid.*, 185.

19. Grylls, *Mary Shelley*, p. 298. For the dating, see p. 301 n.

20. Gisborne, p. 165.

21. Shelley, *Letters*, II, 435.

22. *Ibid.*, II, 218. (This postscript, to a letter of Mary's, was first published in 1955).

23. *Lives of . . . France*, II, 52–53 n. Cf. Mary's letter to Claire of August 12, 1845: "I have been pursued all my life by lowness of spirits which superinduces a certain irritability which often spoils me as a companion" (*Letters*, II, 250).

24. *Letters*, I, 198.

25. *Journal*, pp. 181–82.

26. Wolfe, I, 5. (Hogg printed this for the first time in the preface to his biography of Shelley.)

27. *Journal*, p. 185.

28. *Letters*, I, 187.

29. "Nov. 11," *Journal*, pp. 185–86 (entry date corrected from Nitchie, *Mary Shelley*, p. 50 n.).

30. *Letters*, I, 341.

31. Mrs. Marshall, II, 149.

32. Nitchie, "Shelley at Eton," pp. 48–49.

33. *Letters*, I, 264.

34. This picture, of course, is not the whole one of Shelley. But it is surely an essential part of the man and the husband, regardless of how much his poetry transcended his human limitations.

35. Sylva Norman, *The Flight of the Skylark* (Norman, 1954), p. 64.

36. *Letters*, I, 272.

37. *Ibid.*, 287. See Nitchie, *Mary Shelley*, pp. 63–66, for the known articles during this period.

38. Godwin to Mary, February 27, 1824: "As to the idea that you have no literary talent, for God's sake, do not give way to such diseased imaginations" (Marshall, II, 108).

39. *Journal*, p. 193. See also Chapter 1, Section IV.

40. *Ibid.*, p. 194.

41. *Letters*, I, 291–92.

42. See, for example, the entry for October 19, 1822 (*Journal*, pp. 183–84).

43. On July 9, Mary went to a private viewing of Byron's body (*Letters*, I, 197).

44. *Journal*, p. 195.

45. See *Letters*, II, 347–53 (Appendix II), for a concise and sympathetic account of Mary's "romantic" activities during this period; for an unsympathetic view, see *The Romance of Mary Wollstonecraft Shelley, John Howard Payne and Washington Irving* (Boston, 1907), especially pp. 10, 16, 27–28, 32–61.

46. Sylva Norman, ed. *After Shelley* (London, 1938), p. 61.

47. The material dealing with the initial reviews of *The Last Man* is drawn from Nitchie, *Mary Shelley*, pp. 151–52.

48. Mrs. Marshall, II, 149–50.

49. Norman, *Flight of the Skylark*, p. 62 n. For other discussions of the common theme during the period, see Spark, *Child of Light*, pp. 164–65; and Nitchie, *Mary Shelley*, p. 152.

50. Mary's first published piece was a paragraph which assessed Cobbett as a dangerous man (*Letters*, I, 37, 41 n.).

51. *Child of Light*, p. 153.

52. *Mary Shelley*, pp. 14–15.

53. Unpublished journal entry cited in Nitchie, *Mary Shelley*, pp. 14–15.

54. A. C. Bradley, *Oxford Lectures on Poetry* (Bloomington, 1961 reprint), p. 141.

55. Herbert Lindenberger, *On Wordsworth's Prelude* (Princeton, 1963), p. 211.

56. Shelley's political theory is, of course, much more complex than Ryland's (or Adrian's). However, it seems to me undeniable that Ryland represents something of Mary's concept of the pragmatic working out of Shelley's theories. Furthermore, Mary's departure from Shelley's most elaborate statement of his political theories, "A Philosophical View of Reform" is surely indicated both by her refusal to publish the essay in her lifetime and in her suggestive deviations from Shelley's text in her transcription of the manuscript (see *Shelley's Prose,* pp. 240–41).

57. Edmund Burke, *Reflections on the French Revolution,* eds. W. Alison Phillips and Catherine Beatrice Phillips (Cambridge, England, 1912), p. 51.

58. For a brilliant account of the transformation of the idea of "culture" into an antiegalitarian rallying point, see Raymond Williams, *Culture and Society: 1780–1950* (New York, 1966 reprint).

59. Burke, *Reflections,* p. 79.

60. *Journal,* p. 197.

61. *Letters,* II, 317–18.

62. *Lives of . . . France,* I, 12.

63. *Ibid.,* II, 308. But cf. somewhat conflicting ideas in Mary's sketch of Madame Roland, *ibid.,* II, 265, 290.

64. *Rambles,* I, 143–44. This remark, however, should be compared to Mary's analysis of the unhappy effects of a condition of near-equality in Florence, *ibid.,* II, 183.

65. *Journal,* p. 197.

66. Spark, *Child of Light,* p. 191.

67. Norman, "Mary Shelley: Novelist," pp. 56–57.

68. Lovell, *Keats-Shelley Journal,* p. 49 n.

69. Norman, "Mary Shelley: Novelist," p. 62.

70. *Letters,* II, 313–14.

Chapter Five

1. *Proserpine and Midas,* ed. A. Koszul (London, 1922), p. xi.

2. Gareth W. Dunleavy, "Two New Mary Shelley Letters," *Keats-Shelley Journal,* XIII (1964), 6–11. See also *Letters,* II, 7, 11, 15.

3. Unpublished journal entry of June 7, 1836, quoted in Nitchie, *Mary Shelley,* p. 171 n. Cf. Trelawny, *Letters,* p. 201.

4. *Letters,* II, 196.

5. *Ibid.,* I, 371.

6. *Ibid.,* II, 28.

7. *The Fortunes of Perkin Warbeck* (London, 1830), I, 1. The date is misprinted as "1415" in this, the first edition.

8. See also the journal entry for October 21, 1838 (the year should, perhaps, be 1831): "I like society; I believe all persons who have any talent . . . do" (*Journal,* p. 205).

9. I have expanded upon an insight of Muriel Spark's (*Child of Light*, p. 171).

10. Dowden, I, 436. Dowden provides a three-page analysis of some of the biographic elements (I, 436–38). See also his letter to Richard Garnett, July 31, 1885, on the same score, *Letters about Shelley*, ed. R. Garnett (London, 1917), pp. 139–41. And cf. Mary's own letter to Maria Gisborne, October 13, 1835. *Letters*, II, 109.

11. Norman, "Mary Shelley: Novelist," p. 72.

12. *Shelley and Mary*, III, 1161.

13. *Letters*, II, 72; "Eight Letters by Mary Wollstonecraft Shelley," ed. Elizabeth Nitchie, *Keats-Shelley Memorial Bulletin*, III (1950), 28–29. But see also *Letters*, II, 83.

14. *Letters*, II, 78, 86, 90, 101.

15. *Lodore* (1835), p. 30.

16. *Rambles*, II, 190.

17. "Eight Letters by Mary Wollstonecraft Shelley," ed. Nitchie, p. 29. The remark is applied to Cornelia, Lodore's widow, but see the subsection devoted to *Falkner*.

18. *Lives of . . . France*, II, 327.

19. An amusing instance of the inexactness of *Lodore* as a title is the rechristening of the novel in the pirated edition published in Philadelphia (probably in the 1870's) by T. B. Peterson & Brothers; the title is *The Beautiful Widow*.

20. *Letters*, II, 106, 108.

21. *Falkner* (1837), I, 47.

22. Mary furnished Trelawny with extensive editorial assistance on the *Adventures* and saw it through the press for him.

23. See Nitchie, *Mary Shelley*, pp. 123–26; see also *Letters*, II, 120 n.

24. Cited in Marchand, *Byron*, III, 963.

25. See n. 11, Chapter 4.

26. *Letters*, II, 97.

27. Spark, *Child of Light*, p. 164.

28. *Mathilda*, p. x.

29. Less than a week after Mary finished the first draft on *Mathilda*, she wrote to Amelia Curran, September 18, 1819: "I have no consolation in any quarter, for my misfortune has not altered the tone of my father's letters" (*Letters*, I, 79). For an example of the coldness of Godwin's tone, see his letter to Mary, October 27, 1818, in Mrs. Marshall, I, 229; cf. Elizabeth Nitchie's summary of the situation, *Mary Shelley*, pp. 92–93.

30. Nitchie, *Mary Shelley*, pp. 211–12; White, *Shelley*, II, 39–56; Jones, ed., Shelley, *Letters*, II, 41 n.; Kenneth Neill Cameron, *"Mathilda"* (review), *Keats-Shelley Journal*, X (1961), 113.

31. Gisborne, pp. 43–44.

32. At one point (pp. 66 ff.) Woodville argues against suicide in a fashion

that runs back, through Godwin, to the earl of Shaftesbury at the opening of the eighteenth century.

33. To Maria Gisborne, November 16, 1819, Shelley, *Letters,* II, 156. The continuation of this letter is important for showing the difference between *Mathilda* and *The Cenci* in the fundamental treatment of incest: "It [incest] may be the excess of love or of hate. It may be that defiance of every thing for the sake of another which clothes itself in the glory of the highest heroism, or it may be that cynical rage which confounding the good & bad in existing opinions breaks through them for the purpose of rioting in selfishness & antipathy."

34. "The Heir of Mondolfo" is currently available in a paperback anthology (see the Selected Bibliography). Sixteen other short stories (as well as Claire Clairmont's "The Pole") are found in *Tales and Stories,* ed. Garnett.

35. *Tales and Stories,* p. 148.

36. Bradford A. Booth, "The Pole: A story by Claire Clairmont," *English Literary History,* V (1938), 69 n.

37. *Midas* contains a number of defective lines (see *Proserpine and Midas,* p. 61 n.). Interestingly, Sylva Norman suggests that the play may actually be the product of (at the least) a collaboration with Edward Williams ("Mary Shelley: Novelist," p. 93); but Mary's letter to Alaric Watts, May 14, 1832, surely indicates that aside from Shelley's two lyrics *Midas* is her own (*Letters,* II, 59 & n.). And see Medwin, *Shelley,* p. 252.

38. The poem heads the notes to the poetry of 1822.

39. *Letters,* II, 98.

40. Although H. Buxton Forman first published "The Choice" in a private edition of 1876, I have used the text printed in Grylls, *Mary Shelley,* pp. 297–301, which collates an earlier version with Forman's text.

41. *Letters,* II, 98 n. Some of Mary's other poetry can be conveniently found in Grylls, *Mary Shelley,* pp. 302–4; Nitchie, *Mary Shelley,* pp. 231–35; and Norman, "Mary Shelley: Novelist," pp. 87–88.

42. *Letters,* II, 98.

43. I have cited the earlier text of the poem, found most conveniently in *Letters,* II, 99–100. The revised text can be found in Shelley, *Poems,* p. 675.

44. See Norman, "Mary Shelley: Novelist," p. 89.

Chapter Six

1. *Letters,* II, 196.

2. *Ibid.,* II, 206–7, 209.

3. Norman, *Flight of the Skylark,* p. 161; Elizabeth Nitchie, "Mary Shelley, Traveler," *Keats-Shelley Journal,* X (1961), 34; Nitchie, *Mary Shelley,* pp. 177–78.

4. Jones, ed., *Letters*, II, 156 n. See also Nitchie, "Mary Shelley, Traveler," p. 32; and Spark, *Child of Light*, p. 126. (The exception from praising the *Rambles* is Sylva Norman, *Flight of the Skylark*, pp. 161–62.)

5. The only serious rival to the pain Mary suffered in 1845 would seem to be her anguish in 1827–28 over Jane Williams' tale-bearing concerning Shelley's unhappiness with Mary and his infatuation with Jane in the last months of his life (see *Journal*, p. 198 & n.; *Letters*, I, 368 & n.).

6. See *Letters*, II, 193–94 n., II, 251 ff.

7. *Letters*, II, 252.

8. Cited in Grylls, *Mary Shelley*, p. 275. Perhaps significantly, the entry is dated October 2, 1844, when Mary was evidently becoming more and more involved, financially and (no doubt) emotionally with Gatteschi.

9. *Letters*, II, 258.

10. See Norman, *Flight of the Skylark*, p. 161 & n.

11. See also, in the *Rambles*, I, 131, 169; II, 77–78, 81.

12. *Letters*, II, 224.

13. *Ibid.*, 226.

14. *Ibid.*, 254.

15. Professor Jones, ed., *Letters*, II, 194 n., would also credit Gatteschi with Letter 20, "The Pontifical States." But, while it is reasonably certain that Gatteschi did give Mary some help with her background details on Rome, she also mentions, in the *Rambles*, "several" persons as her source of information concerning the cholera outbreak at Rome in 1837 (II, 236); and she alludes to an "English gentleman" who recounted his experiences to her (II, 239). It should be added that another area where Gatteschi's help seems to be evident is in Letter 15, dealing with Tuscany.

16. *Letters*, II, 196.

17. Cited in Norman, *Flight of the Skylark*, p. 162.

18. Elizabeth Nitchie, "Mary Shelley, Traveler," *Keats-Shelley Journal* (1961).

19. See above, Chapter 1, Section II, Mary touches upon Louvet briefly in *Lives . . . France*, II, 284. (For Wordsworth's mention of him in *The Prelude*, see Book X, 11. 9–120.)

20. William H. Marshall, *Byron . . . and The Liberal*, p. 174, ascribes this article to Mary on sound grounds. It may be found in *The Liberal*, II, 67–83.

21. See above, Chapter 4, Section II. Another article, that on Giovanni Villani published in *The Liberal*, is less biographical than descriptive of Villani's chronical history.

22. See above, Chapter 4, Section I.

23. *Letters*, I, 313 n.

24. *Ibid.*, II, 10 n.

25. *Ibid.*, 20.

26. Although Murray was never to commit himself to any of Mary's literary proposals, she began serious research on Madame de Staël by

March 5, 1830, at the latest; and she evidently discarded her interest in Empress Josephine by May 25 to concentrate on Madame de Staël alone (see *Letters,* II, 31, 32, 33–34).

27. *Letters,* II, 34–35.

28. See Paul, I, 81–83. 332–33 (on Maria Gisborne [as Mrs. Reveley]); I, 231–32 (on Mary's mother); I, 76, 79–80, 161–62, 238–39 (on Godwin); I, 47 (on James Marshall); I, 78–79 (on Thomas Wedgwood).

29. *Letters,* II, 92–93.

30. *Ibid.,* 200.

31. *Ibid.,* 83.

32. *Ibid.,* 122.

33. *Ibid.,* 106, 108. Brewster also wrote volume XIX in the *Cabinet Cyclopedia* dealing with optics.

34. Both the format and the style of the Ercilla sketch (103–19) are noticeably different from the other work in the *Cyclopedia* which we know to be Mary's. In format, the essay on Ercilla makes use of two pages of end notes (no other sketch does), and the style itself seems markedly heavier than anything in the other essays.

35. Norman, "Mary Shelley: Novelist," p. 79. Both Nitchie (*Mary Shelley,* p. 160) and Spark (*Child of Light,* p. 126) speak highly of the *Lives.*

36. However, when such matters have seemed to be of significance for a better understanding of Mary Shelley's work, I have not avoided touching upon them. See especially Chapter 4, Section I, Chapter 5, Section II.

37. Joseph Raben, "Shelley's 'Invocation to Misery,'" *Journal of English and Germanic Philology,* LXV (1966), 65.

38. Aside from a relatively small number of exceptions (the most notable being the expansion of *Queen Mab,* and the inclusion of *Peter Bell the Third* and *Swellfoot the Tyrant*), the second edition of 1839 (in one volume) relies on the four-volume edition for its textual basis.

39. Charles H. Taylor, Jr., *The Early Collected Editions of Shelley's Poems* (New-Haven, 1958), pp. 44–45. The corruptions were magnified because of a subsequent failure to take note of the errata leaf in the *Posthumous Poems.* (See also Taylor's article in *Publications of the Modern Language Association,* LXX [June 1955], 408–16.)

40. Taylor, *Early Collected Editions,* p. 45.

41. *Letters,* II, 10 & n.

42. See Raben's article, especially pp. 65–66; but cf. Irving Massey's "Shelley's 'Music, When Soft Voices Die,'" *Journal of English and Germanic Philology,* LIX (1960), 430–38, for an indication that Mary's alterations were occasionally haphazard or gratuitous.

43. Even Raben, one of Mary's severest critics, concedes this (p. 67 n.). Furthermore, the fact that Moxon *was* prosecuted for publishing all of *Queen Mab* in the second edition of 1839 should be sufficient proof that Mary often had justifiable reasons for her suppressions.

44. Neville Rogers, "The Punctuation of Shelley's Syntax," *Keats-Shelley Memorial Bulletin,* XVII (1966), 25.

45. Wolfe, II, 197.

46. Shelley, *Poems,* p. 676 n. Hereafter, all citations from the prefaces and notes to the poetry will be made in the body of the text.

47. *Journal,* pp. 206–7.

48. *Journal,* p. 208.

49. See, for example, *Letters,* I, 206, 264, 281, 292; II, 126–127, 129, 133, 150; Taylor, *Early Collected Editions,* p. 45; Massey, "The First Edition," pp. 29–38.

50. *Letters,* II, 139; see also I, 286.

51. Herbert Read, *A Coat of Many Colours* (New York, 1956), pp. 123–24.

52. Norman, *Flight of the Skylark,* p. 144.

53. Mary does refer to the "Lord Chancellor" poem in her note on the poems of 1817, but she slides away from the hatred within it and makes much of "the tenderness of a father's love" which is also evidenced within the poem (Shelley, *Poems,* 551).

54. Read, *Coat of Many Colours,* p. 119.

55. *Letters,* II, 28.

Selected Bibliography

This listing is highly selective. A much fuller bibliography of Mary Shelley's works may be found in Elizabeth Nitchie's *Mary Shelley*, pp. 205–10, to which add "Madame D'Houtetot," *The Liberal,* II, 67–83, and a thirty-three page fragment of a novel (about a boy named Cecil) in Lord Abinger's collection.

PRIMARY SOURCES

1. *Novels*

Falkner. 3 vols. London: Saunders and Otley, 1837.

The Fortunes of Perkin Warbeck. 3 vols. London: Henry Colburn and Richard Bentley, 1830.

Frankenstein; or the Modern Prometheus, ed. Harold Bloom. New York: The New American Library, "Signet Classics," 1965. This edition, based on a copy of the "third" edition of 1831 in the Carl H. Pforzheimer Library, is the source of all quotations in the text. For a fuller bibliographical discussion of *Frankenstein* see above, n. 24, Chapter 2.

The Last Man, ed. Hugh J. Luke, Jr. Lincoln: University of Nebraska Press, 1965.

Lodore. New York: Wallis & Newell, 1835.

Valperga: or, the Life and Adventures of Castruccio, Prince of Lucca. 3 vols. London: G. and W. B. Whittaker, 1823.

2. *Shorter Fiction and Verse*

"The Choice." *Mary Shelley.* Ed. R. Glynn Grylls. London: Oxford University Press, 1938.

"The Heir of Mondolfo." *Seven Masterpieces of Gothic Horror.* Ed. Robert Donald Spector. New York: Bantam Books, 1963.

Mathilda. Ed. Elizabeth Nitchie. *Studies in Philology, Extra Series,* No. 3. Chapel Hill: University of North Carolina Press, 1959.

Proserpine and Midas: Two Unpublished Mythological Dramas. Ed. A. Koszul. London: Humphrey Milford, 1922.

Tales and Stories. Ed. Richard Garnett. London: William Paterson & Co., 1891.

"The Trial of Love." *The Keepsake for 1835*. Ed. Frederick Mansel Rey-
    nolds. London: Longman, Rees, Orme, Brown, Green, and Longmans,
    1835.

3. *Nonfiction (including the letters and journal)*

"Eight Letters by Mary Wollstonecraft Shelley." Ed. Elizabeth Nitchie.
    Keats-Shelley Memorial Bulletin, III (1950), 23–32.
*History of a Six Weeks' Tour through a Part of France, Switzerland, Ger-
    many, and Holland: with Letters Descriptive of a Sail Round the Lake
    of Geneva, and of the Glaciers of Chamouni*. London: T. Hookham
    and C. and J. Ollier, 1817.
Journal. (See below, *Mary Shelley's Journal*.)
The Letters of Mary W. Shelley. Ed. Frederick L. Jones. 2 vols. Norman:
    University of Oklahoma Press, 1946.
Lives of the Most Eminent Literary and Scientific Men of France. 2 vols.
    London: Longman, Orme, Brown, Green, Longmans, and John
    Taylor, 1838–39. These volumes are nos. 105 and 117 in Lardner's
    Cabinet Cyclopedia (133 vols., 1829–46).
*Lives of the Most Eminent Literary and Scientific Men of Italy, Spain, and
    Portugal*. 3 vols. London: Longman, Brown, Green, and Longmans,
    1835–37. These volumes are nos. 63, 71, and 96 in Lardner's.
Mary Shelley's Journal. Ed. Frederick L. Jones. Norman: University of
    Oklahoma Press, 1947.
"Mary Shelley to Maria Gisborne: New Letters, 1818–1822." Ed. Frederick
    L. Jones. *Studies in Philology*, LII (1955), 39–74.
Preface. *Essays, Letters from Abroad, Translations and Fragments*, by
    Percy Bysshe Shelley. 2 vols. London: Edward Moxon, 1840.
Preface (s) and Notes. *The Complete Poetical Works of Percy Bysshe Shelley*.
    Ed. Thomas Hutchinson. London: Oxford University Press reprint,
    1965. This edition contains the texts of the prefaces and notes written
    by Mary for her editions of Shelley's poetry.
Rambles in Germany and Italy in 1840, 1842, and 1843. 2 vols. London:
    Edward Moxon, 1844.

SECONDARY SOURCES

1. *Books*

BOAS, LOUISE SCHUTZ. *Harriet Shelley: Five Long Years*. London: Uni-
    versity Press, 1962. Interesting, sympathetic account of Shelley's
    first wife; marred at times by undue reliance on a discredited book,
    Robert Metcalf Smith's *The Shelley Legend* (see below).
BROWN, FORD K. *The Life of William Godwin*. London; J. M. Dent & Sons,
    Ltd., 1926. Still probably the best biography of Mary's father.

CAMERON, KENNETH NEILL, ed. *Shelley and His Circle.* Vols. 1–4. Cambridge: Harvard University Press, 1961, 1970. Contains material on Mary Shelley, Claire Clairmont, William Godwin, Shelley, and Mary Wollstonecraft not found elsewhere. Volume III of this projected eight-volume edition of material in Carl H. Pforzheimer Library includes Sylva Norman's most recent assessment of Mary's life and work.

———. *The Young Shelley: Genesis of a Radical.* New York: The Crowell-Collier Publishing Co., Collier Book reprint, 1962. Essential study of Shelley's development down to 1814, the year in which he eloped with Mary.

CHURCH, RICHARD. *Mary Shelley.* London: Gerald Howe, Ltd., 1928. An uneven book, to be used with care. Of value on *Frankenstein,* it is very weak on the other writings and contains some glaring errors (e.g., Adrian as the final survivor in *The Last Man*).

CLAIRMONT, CLAIRE. *The Journals of Claire Clairmont.* Ed. Marion Kingston Stocking. Cambridge: Harvard University Press, 1968. Valuable glimpses of Mary and Shelley from their close companion.

DOWDEN, EDWARD. *The Life of Percy Bysshe Shelley.* 2 vols. London: Kegan Paul, Trench & Co., 1886. Although supplanted by White's *Shelley* (see below) as the standard life, still of value.

GISBORNE, MARIA, EDWARD E. WILLIAMS. *Shelley's Friends: Their Journals and Letters.* Ed. Frederick L. Jones. Norman: University of Oklahoma Press, 1951. Much of interest, especially concerning Shelley's last days and the Gisbornes' contacts with the Godwins in 1820.

GRYLLS, R[OSALIE] G. *Mary Shelley: A Biography.* London: Oxford University Press, 1938. Some errors, but still the best biography.

INGPEN, ROGER. *Shelley in England.* Boston and New York: Houghton Mifflin Co., 1917. Contains material relating to Shelley, Mary and Harriet not found elsewhere.

The Liberal: Verse and Prose from the South. 2 vols. London: John Hunt, 1822–23. The four numbers of the ill-fated periodical to which Mary was a contributor. (See William H. Marshall, below.)

MARCHAND, LESLIE. *Byron.* 3 vols. New York: Alfred A. Knopf, 1957. Standard biography.

MARSHALL, MRS. JULIAN. *The Life & Letters of Mary Wollstonecraft Shelley.* 2 vols. London: Richard Bentley & Son, 1889. Written under Lady Shelley's more or less direct guidance, this still contains much of value.

MARSHALL, WILLIAM H. *Byron, Shelley, Hunt, and The Liberal.* Philadelphia: University of Pennsylvania Press, 1960. Covers, among much else of importance dealing with *The Liberal,* Mary's three contributions.

MEDWIN, THOMAS. *The Life of Percy Bysshe Shelley.* Ed. H. Buxton Forman. London: Oxford University Press, 1913. Often erroneous in detail, but still of value for firsthand impressions.

MOORE, THOMAS. *Letters and Journals of Lord Byron: With Notices of His Life.* 2 vols. London: John Murray, 1830. The account of Byron at Geneva in 1816 draws upon Mary's recollections.

NITCHIE, ELIZABETH. *Mary Shelley: Author of Frankenstein.* New Brunswick: Rutgers University Press, 1953. Indispensable for the student of Mary Shelley.

NORMAN, SYLVA, ed. *After Shelley: The Letters of Thomas Jefferson Hogg to Jane Williams.* London: Oxford University Press, 1938. Valuable side glimpses of Mary.

————. *The Flight of the Skylark: The Development of Shelley's Reputation.* Norman: University of Oklahoma Press, 1954. Amusing, well-written book with much information on Mary's widowhood not found elsewhere.

PAUL, C. KEGAN. *William Godwin: His Friends and Contemporaries.* 2 vols. Boston: Roberts Brothers, 1876. Erroneous and pedestrian, but the letters and manuscript records it reprints—along with some highly interesting notes on Godwin and Mary Wollstonecraft by Mary herself—still have great value.

SCOTT, WALTER S., ed. *New Shelley Letters.* New Haven: Yale University Press, 1949. Rather slovenly edition of important letters, including some still not found elsewhere. (The letters appeared earlier in three separate volumes, each edited by Scott, with fuller annotation.)

Shelley and Mary. Eds. Sir Percy Shelley and Lady Jane Shelley. 3 [or 4] vols. Privately printed, 1882. Much of the material in this more than twelve-hundred-page compilation of letters and journals is now available elsewhere. The serious student, however, will want to acquaint himself with the arrangement and contents of this no longer extremely rare compilation—thanks to the convenience of microfilm. (Since the pages are numbered consecutively throughout, there is no difficulty presented by citations from either the three-volume or four-volume set.)

SHELLEY, PERCY BYSSHE. *The Complete Poetical Works.* . . . Ed. Thomas Hutchinson. London: Oxford University Press reprint, 1965. (Cited as *Poems.*) Reliable texts for almost all of Shelley's poetry, as well as for all of Mary's preface and notes to it.

————. *The Letters.* . . . Ed. Frederick L. Jones. 2 vols. Oxford: The Clarendon Press, 1964. The standard edition, with unusually helpful annotation.

————. *Shelley's Prose: or, The Trumpet of a Prophecy.* Ed. David Lee Clark. 2nd ed. Albuquerque: University of New Mexico Press, 1966. Contains most of the prose, often with useful annotations.

SMITH, ROBERT METCALF, in collaboration with MARTHA MARY SCHLEGEL, THEODORE GEORGE EHRSAM, and LOUISE ADDISON WATERS. *The Shelley Legend.* New York: Charles Scribner's Sons, 1945. Although not without value, this book is guilty of such extreme distortions, exaggerations, and downright errors that the student should not use it until he has thoroughly acquainted himself with *An Examination of the Shelley Legend* (see below, White *et al.*).

SPARK, MURIEL. *Child of Light: A Reassessment of Mary Wollstonecraft Shelley*. Hadleigh: Essex, England: Tower Bridge Publications, 1951. Sensitive, sympathetic, and well written, this is especially valuable for its analyses of *Frankenstein, The Last Man,* and *Perkin Warbeck*. An abridgment of *The Last Man* is included at the end of the volume.

TAYLOR, CHARLES H., JR. *The Early Collected Editions of Shelley's Poems: A Study in the History and Transmission of the Printed Text*. New Haven: Yale University Press, 1958. Essential for any study of Mary as Shelley's editor.

TRELAWNY, EDWARD JOHN. *The Letters . . .,* ed. H. Buxton Forman. London: Oxford University Press, 1910. Reflects an increasingly hostile view of Mary.

WHITE, NEWMAN IVEY. *Shelley*. 2 vols. New York: Alfred A. Knopf, 1940. Standard biography.

―――. Jones, FREDERICK L. and KENNETH NEILL CAMERON. *An Examination of "The Shelley Legend."* Philadelphia: University of Pennsylvania Press, 1951. A reprinting in single-volume form of three separate critiques of Robert Metcalf Smith's *The Shelley Legend* (see above). The three critiques may be found separately as follows: White, *"The Shelley Legend Examined,"*. *Studies in Philology*, XLIII (1946), 422–14; Jones, "The Shelley Legend," *Publications of the Modern Language Association*, LXI (1946), 848–90; Cameron, "A New Shelley Legend," *Journal of English and Germanic Philology*, XLV (1946), 369–79.

WOLFE, HUMBERT, ed. *The Life of Percy Bysshe Shelley as Comprised in "The Life of Shelley" by Thomas Jefferson Hogg; "The Recollections of Shelley & Byron" by Edward John Trelawny; "Memoirs of Shelley" by Thomas Love Peacock*. 2 vols. London: J. M. Dent and Sons, 1933. Three views of Shelley by men who knew him.

2. Articles

BLOOM, HAROLD. Afterword, *Frankenstein* (Signet edition), pp. 212–23 (see above, Primary Source). Stimulating discussion of the novel from what is essentially a neo-Kierkegaardian point of view (the "novel's prime theme is a necessary counterpoise to Prometheanism, for Prometheanism exalts the increase in consciousness at all cost"). Reprinted in *Partisan Review*, XXXII, 4 (Fall, 1965), 611–18.

DUNLEAVY, GARETH W. "Two New Mary Shelley Letters and the 'Irish' Chapters of *Perkin Warbeck*," *Keats-Shelley Journal*, XIII (1964), 6–11. Valuable for demonstrating Mary's extended interest in her fourth novel.

GOLDBERG, M. A. "Moral and Myth in Mrs. Shelley's *Frankenstein,*" *Keats-Shelley Journal,* VIII, Part I (1959), 27–38. Perhaps the single most helpful article on the novel, particularly in relating it to the moral and social thought of the time.

LOVELL, ERNEST J., JR. "Byron and the Byronic Hero in the Novels of Mary Shelley," *The University of Texas Studies in English,* XXX (1951), 158–83. Byron as the prototype of major figures in *Valperga* (Castruccio), *The Last Man* (Raymond), *Lodore* (Lodore), and *Falkner* (Falkner).

————. "Byron and Mary Shelley," *Keats-Shelley Journal,* II (1953), 35–49. Mary's interest in Byron, a good deal of it unconscious, as "father, foster father, husband . . . [and] lover of a dependent Mary" (p.36). Persuasive, humane, and thoroughly unsentimental.

MASSEY, IRVING. "The First Edition of *Shelley's Poetical Works* (1839): Some Manuscript Sources," *Keats-Shelley Journal,* XVI (1967), 29–38. Altogether, this article tends to give Mary a somewhat higher mark in reliability and conscientiousness as an editor than has lately been argued.

MILLHOUSER, MILTON. "The Noble Savage in Mary Shelley's *Frankenstein,*" *Notes and Queries,* CXC (January–June, 1946), 248–50. Contends that the characterization of the monster becomes confused by the intrusion of the "noble savage" concept into an originally sinister theme.

NELSON, LOWRY, JR. "Night Thoughts on the Gothic Novel," *Yale Review,* LII (Winter 1963), 236–57. Includes an assessment of the contribution made by *Frankenstein* to the genre.

NITCHIE, ELIZABETH. "Shelley at Eton: Mary Shelley vs. Jefferson Hogg," *Keats-Shelley Memorial Bulletin,* XI (1960), 48–54. Brief account of Mary's early effort to write Shelley's life, a description of the manuscript fragment which survives, and an analysis of Hogg's butchering of the original material in his own biography of Shelley.

————. "Mary Shelley, Traveler," *Keats-Shelley Journal,* X (1961) 29–42. Evaluation of Mary's travel writings, with the greatest emphasis placed on her last published work, *Rambles in Germany and Italy.*

NORMAN, SYLVA. "Mary Shelley: Novelist and Dramatist." *On Shelley.* London: Oxford University Press, 1938. Valuable, but perhaps a little too ready to score points off Mary's weaknesses as a writer.

————. "Mary Wollstonecraft Shelley." *Shelley and His Circle.* Ed. Kenneth Neill Cameron, III (Cambridge, Mass.: Harvard University Press, 1970), 397–422. Sylva Norman's most recent assessment of Mary. A valuable over-all treatment.

PECK, WALTER EDWIN. "The Biographical Element in the Novels of Mary Wollstonecraft Shelley," *Publications of the Modern Language Associ-*

ation, XXXVIII (1923), 196–219. An early effort to pursue Dowden's reading of *Lodore* by investigating the other novels for biographical details concerning Shelley, Byron, Claire, Godwin, and so forth. Peck's two-volume biography of Shelley (1927) added nothing to the contentions of the article.

RABEN, JOSEPH. "Shelley's 'Invocation to Misery': An Expanded Text," *Journal of English and Germanic Philology,* LXV (1966), 65–74. Examination of Mary's manipulation of Shelley's text.

RIEGER, JAMES. "Dr. Polidori and the Genesis of *Frankenstein,*" *Studies in English Literature,* III (1963), 461–472. Reexamination of Mary's account in the 1831 introduction to *Frankenstein* describing the novel's composition; several errors and discrepancies pointed out.

———. "Shelley's Paterin Beatrice," *Studies in Romanticism,* IV (Autumn, 1964–Summer, 1965), 169–84. Relationship between the Beatrice of Mary's *Valperga* and the Beatrice of *The Cenci.*

SPARK, MURIEL. "Mary Shelley: A Prophetic Novelist," *The Listener,* XLV (February 22, 1951), 305–6. Some aspects of the contemporary relevance of *Frankenstein* and *The Last Man.*

Index

DATE DUE

6	FEB 3 '81		
9 '81			
MAR.25 '81	APR 6 '81		
FEB. 2 4 1993	FB 23 93		
GAYLORD			PRINTED IN U.S.A.